Folens

Book 2

LANGUAGE WORKS

Contents

Skeletons in the Stones

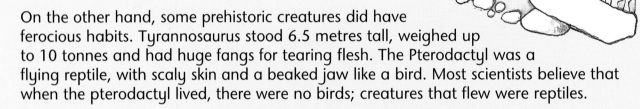

Dinosaurs were giant reptiles that roamed the Earth millions of years ago, long before humans lived. When people think of a prehistoric animal, they usually picture in their minds a ferocious beast with huge teeth and massive claws, tearing its victims to pieces with blood-curdling roars! However, not all creatures were like that and some of the largest and most interesting were quite timid animals, who ate nothing more than plants and grasses. In fact, if you think about it, most of the large animals alive today – horses, cattle, elephants, giraffes – eat no flesh, but are all vegetarians.

On the other hand, some prehistoric creatures did have ferocious habits. Tyrannosaurus stood 6.5 metres tall, weighed up to 10 tonnes and had huge fangs for tearing flesh. The Pterodactyl was a flying reptile, with scaly skin and a beaked jaw like a bird. Most scientists believe that when the pterodactyl lived, there were no birds; creatures that flew were reptiles.

The name 'dinosaur' was first used in books by Sir Richard Owen in 1842. He and other scientists discovered that the fossils they were studying were not from any group of animals alive at the time. Sir Richard decided to call them by a new name. He took two Greek words *deinos*, which means 'terrible', and *sauros*, which means 'lizard'. So the actual meaning of the word dinosaur is 'terrible lizard'. In 1842 the word terrible meant terrifying or frightening.

Dinosaurs lived on the Earth from about 230 million to 65 million years ago, a total time of 165 million years. So far scientists have discovered over 350 different species (types). Over 150 of these have only been discovered in the last 20 years. There may be many more to find still hidden in the ground.

The Natural History Museum in London has a skeleton of a very unusual dinosaur: Archaeopteryx. This animal had many of the features of a dinosaur, but it also had feathers. Scientists believe therefore that another dinosaur was able to fly.

In the past the Chinese used a word called 'konglong' to describe the enormous bones that they dug from the ground. The word means both dinosaur and terrible dragon. Long ago, many people believed in dragons, so when a Chinese farmer dug these bones from the ground, he believed he had found the remains of a dragon. In those days a dragon was believed to bring good luck so the farmer would take the bone, grind it into powder and eat it so that he would be lucky.

Answer these questions.

1. What were the dinosaurs?
2. What do people imagine when they think of a prehistoric animal?
3. What are vegetarians?
4. What was a Tyrannosaurus?
5. What was a pterodactyl?
6. How long did the dinosaurs live on Earth?
7. Why do scientists think that Archaeopteryx could fly?
8. Explain the link between the dinosaur and the dragon.

 Read 'Skeletons in the Stones' again.

1. Write a heading for each paragraph of 'Skeletons in the Stones'.
2. Why would headings be useful? Write down your answer.
3. Make up a new title for the account. Think of interesting words. (Don't call it 'Dinosaurs'!)
4. Remember, a fact is something which is true, fiction is something which is made up and an opinion is someone's point of view.

   Write down a fact, an example of fiction and a point of view from 'Skeletons in the Stones'.

 Find out more about one of the following:

	Tyrannosaurus	pterodactyl	Archaeopteryx
pronounced	(tir-an-o-sawr-us)	(ter-o-dac-til)	(ark-ee-op-ter-ix)

or another dinosaur of your own choice.
You will need to look in the library or use ICT.

 In your own words write two paragraphs about dinosaurs, using information you discover and information from 'Skeletons in the Stones'.

Give each paragraph a heading and think of an interesting title for your account. Remember, you cannot write about everything. You must select some information and leave out the rest.

Confusing Words (1)

A **Write out the sentences, adding the correct words.**

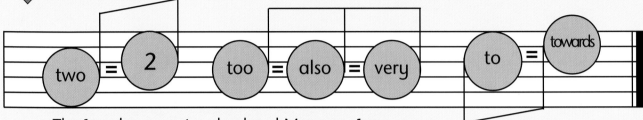

The **two** boys ran to school and Mary ran **too**.

1. I can play _____ musical instruments.
2. After orchestra practice we went _____ the shop.
3. If Anna goes _____ the concert Teresa will go _____.
4. We will go _____ hear you sing.
5. He ran very fast and was _____ tired _____ play.

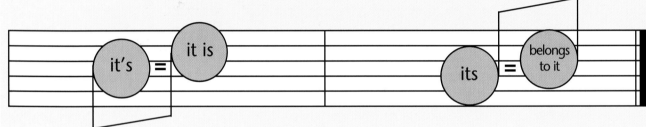

It's in the drawer. The dog stayed in **its** kennel.

6. The violin is in _____ case.
7. _____ a beautiful day for the concert.
8. The tuba rolled over on _____ side.
9. _____ interesting to learn about the orchestra.
10. Take the tambourine out of _____ box because _____ time to start.

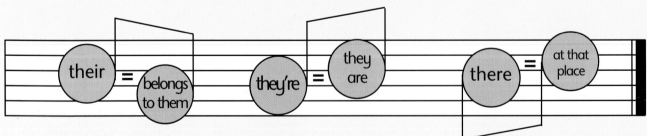

They have lost **their** hats. **They're** outside. My house is over **there**.

11. Mozart's parents were proud of _____ son.
12. _____ leaving for Vienna soon.
13. _____ car is not _____ because _____ on holiday.
14. Salzburg is over _____.
15. _____ lives were full of music.

Capital Letters

- When do we use capital letters?
    1. At the beginning of every sentence.
        e.g. Two skeletons were found.
    2. 'I' when used on its own.
        e.g. I bought a dinosaur poster and I pinned it up on the wall.
    3. For names and titles of people.
        e.g. Professor Chatterjee, Muhammed, Ms Jones, Mary, President Washington.
    4. For titles of things.
        e.g. Tyrannosaurus, Archaeopteryx, Jurassic Park.
    5. For special emphasis.
        e.g. Mum said, "GET OUT OF BED."
    6. For the beginning of new lines in some poetry.

 Write out these sentences, inserting the missing capitals.

1. roald dahl wrote the book 'danny the champion of the world'.
2. steven spielberg directed the film 'jurassic park'.
3. professor chatterjee called the creature 'protoavis'.
4. i saw the film 'the flintstones'.
5. i enjoy reading greek legends.
6. mr orville wright made the first powered flight in 1903.
7. the dinosaur had scaly skin.
8. i asked doctor who to come and see me.
9. i read the book 'matilda' and i've seen the film.

 Write out the passage below, putting in the missing capital letters.

early people probably looked up at the soaring birds. they may have wondered how birds flew and why they could not fly. myths and legends abound with human attempts to imitate the birds. one of the best-known myths is that of daedalus and icarus. daedalus was a brillant greek artist and engineer who built a labyrinth for king minos of crete. the king was so pleased with daedalus' work, however, that he refused to let daedalus leave crete. so daedalus built two sets of wings from feathers stuck together with glue and wax. he and his son icarus hoped to escape from crete with these. the wings worked well until icarus flew too close to the sun. the wax holding the wings together melted. icarus fell into the sea. he drowned. daedalus returned to greece safely. he was grief-stricken at the death of icarus, and vowed never to fly again.

Verbs

- A verb is an 'action' or 'doing' word. It is used to make a statement about a person, place or thing.
- Every sentence must have a verb,

  e.g. **1.** Mount Vesuvius erupted long ago.

  2. Marcus and Julius ran for the city gates.

  3. Pompeii was buried in smouldering black ash.

 Copy the sentences and underline the verbs.

1. He bought a new shirt for the wedding.

2. All the products were scrutinised before leaving the factory.

3. I heard the blackbird singing early in the morning.

4. The student drew a cartoon for the school magazine.

5. The door creaked because the hinge was rusty.

6. The crowd cheered when the team scored a goal.

7. The car turned off the road and overturned in a field.

 Verb search: read the story on page 4 again and list the verbs you see.

were, roamed ...

 Choose the correct verb from the box to complete these sentences.

climbed	retreated	replied	waded	complained	examined

1. The customer _____ to the manager about the item he had bought.

2. The army _____ after the battle.

3. The girls _____ through the water.

4. John _____ the tree in the orchard.

5. The pupil _____ with a correct answer.

6. The doctor _____ the patient carefully.

 Write the opposites to these verbs.

| appear | raise | remember | sold | love |
| break | begin | shut | win | buy |

The B.F.D. (Big Friendly Dinosaur)

 Imagine you have met a flying monster. Despite its fearsome, rugged appearance, it is actually a big friendly dinosaur. The B.F.D. flies you to Dinoland.

1. Write a paragraph describing your journey to Dinoland. Describe how you felt as this gigantic kite of a creature spread and flapped its enormous wings. What did you see around you, below you? How did it feel as it glided and swooped? Did you have a soft landing?

2. Write a paragraph describing what you saw on your arrival in Dinoland. What was it like – the plants, the creatures … ?

3. During your visit you are unfortunate enough to end up inside the mouth of a big ferocious dinosaur. Luckily this B.F.D. hasn't swallowed you. What is it like in there – warm and damp, is its breath smelly, did it need fillings in its teeth? Are they sharp, dangerous, like pillars … ?

4. Write a paragraph explaining how you are rescued. Did the B.F.D. sneeze, burp or bend forward and let you fall out? Did the flying B.F.D. take you under its wing and fly you back home?

Deep Frozen

Nowadays, we know how effective ice is for keeping food from going bad, but until the sixteenth century people only knew how to store food by drying, smoking, salting or pickling. Fruits were dried, milk was made into butter or cheese and grapejuice was made into wine.

At the beginning of winter, people used to have huge feasts; they had to kill most of their animals because there would be no food for the animals to eat until spring. For the rest of the winter the people probably ate very badly.

Long before fridges and freezers had been invented, however, people realised that food could be stored in ice. People living in towns could buy ice from ice-factories, where it was made by a process using salt. Some large country houses had an ice house in the garden, sunk into the ground and lined with bricks where ice could remain frozen for some time.

The man who thought of keeping meat fresh by freezing is said to be Sir Francis Bacon, an English lawyer, philosopher and statesman.

He died in a strange way. One cold wintry day he happened to be in a coach, driving through London with the king's doctor, Dr Witherborne. Snow lay on the ground and Sir Francis had an idea: if meat was buried in the snow, then it would not go bad.

He ordered the coachman to stop, leapt out and ran to a nearby cottage. The woman who lived there owned chickens and he soon persuaded her to sell him one. She killed it, plucked it, drew out its insides and stood in amazement as she saw Sir Francis throw it to the ground and stuff it with snow. Then holding the cold bird, he jumped back into the coach. His great experiment had begun.

However, the wet cold of the snow and the icy wind had proved too much for Sir Francis and he became very ill. He was looked after at a house owned by the Earl of Arundel. Unfortunately, they put him in a bed that had not been slept in for weeks and it was damp. The poor man got worse and within two or three days he was dead.

So, next time you see frozen chicken or ice cream, spare a thought for the unlucky Sir Francis Bacon!

A **Answer these questions.**

1. How did people store food in the sixteenth century?
2. What did they do at the beginning of winter?
3. Where did townspeople get their ice?
4. In large country houses, where was the ice stored?
5. Who thought of freezing meat to keep it fresh?
6. What happened one cold wintry day when Sir Francis was out with Dr Witherborne?
7. How did Sir Francis die?
8. What do you think could happen if the food we eat is not fresh?

 B **Write a newspaper report about an outbreak of food poisoning.**

Before you begin decide:
- what type of illness has occurred
- where it has happened
- who is affected (for example, children or older people)
- how serious it is
- why it has happened.

Write three paragraphs for your report. Think of a suitable newspaper headline and try to write it using the correct style.
Read some newspaper reports to help you.

 C **Find a packet of food (for example, some frozen food or a cake mix) or a tin of food at home.**

Read the instructions and answer these questions.
1. What should happen if you follow the instructions properly?
2. How many things do you have to do? What do you have to do first? Write down the answers.
3. Note all the ingredients in the food. Are there any you don't know? Write them down.
4. Are there any additives or preservatives? If so, what? What are they meant to do? Check in a dictionary.
5. Find out why some people do not like eating additives and preservatives.
   Write whether the instructions are written in the first person 'I', second person 'you' or the third person 'he/she/it'.

Syllables

- When words end in 'y', 'y' says 'ee'. The 'y' uses the consonant before it to make the last syllable.

  e.g. In the sixteenth cen|tu-ry people did not own fridges.

  One cold wint-ry day, Sir Francis was on a coach.

  The i-cy wind proved too much for Sir Francis.

  He was un|luc-ky.

 A **Copy the following words and draw a line between the syllables.**

sil|ly	sor|ry	mis|ty	glossy	clumsy	grumpy	messy
fifty	forty	thirty	seventy	chilly	very	happy
angry	crazy	daisy	nappy	ugly	lucky	particularly
easy	badly	sadly	dandy	scary	simply	unfortunately
dismally	probably	possibly	usually	woolly	eventually	

 B **Use your dictionary to help you find the meaning of these words.**

frequently   fortunately   eventually

probably   easily   century

 C **Make sentences using these words.**

unfortunately
clumsy
thirty
usually
ugly

you are very clumsy

The Full Stop

● Always finish your sentence with a full stop.

 Write out these sentences, putting in the capital letters and full stops.

1. sir francis bacon thought of the idea of freezing meat
2. ice is effective for keeping food fresh
3. sir francis rode through london with dr witherborne
4. there were chickens scratching around the house
5. the doctor ordered that he be taken to the earl's house
6. next time you eat frozen chicken or ice cream, spare a thought for the unlucky sir francis bacon

 There are two sentences in each of the following. Write them out, inserting the full stops and capital letters.

1. snow fell during the night when i awoke i wanted to make a snowman
2. she stood there in amazement he started to stuff the chicken with snow
3. the fridge is a wonderful invention it keeps food fresh
4. huge hairy elephants were called woolly mammoths they were found buried and perfectly preserved
5. we had to stay indoors all day it was too cold to go out and an icy wind was blowing
6. people who lived in towns could get ice from factories it was made by a process using salt
7. the wet snow and icy wind were too much for him he was dead within a few days

 Write out this paragraph and insert all the missing capital letters and full stops.

in prehistoric times there lived huge hairy elephants called woolly mammoths their thick coats kept them warm during the ice age the hump of fat on their backs acted as a foodstore it kept them alive when snow and ice covered the ground they ate grasses, sedges, wild thyme and alpine poppies we know this because they have been discovered in the mouths and stomachs of mammoths they were found buried and perfectly preserved in the frozen soil of siberia their fur, skin and even the blood in their veins were all deep frozen in fact mammoth meat has been preserved really well even after thousands of years it can still be fit to eat

Bear in There

There's a Polar Bear
In our Frigidaire –
He likes it 'cause it's cold in there.
With his seat in the meat
And his face in the fish
And his big hairy paws
In the buttery dish,
He's nibbling the noodles,
He's munching the rice,
He's slurping the soda,
He's licking the ice.
And he lets out a roar
If you open the door.
And it gives me a scare
To know he's in there –
That Polary Bear
In our Frigitydaire.

Shel Silverstein

 Answer these questions.

1. What do people normally call a 'Frigidaire'?

2. What does the poet see in there?

3. Why has the polar bear chosen this particular place?

4. Do you think the bear is comfortable? Give a reason for your answer.

5. What is he doing 'in there'?

6. Is it safe for the poet to open the fridge? How do you know?

7. Do you think this is a good idea for a poem? Why?

 What monster could be in your fridge?

Write down three ideas (such as an icicle monster). Your ideas should be suitable. For instance, a fire monster would be no good in a fridge!

 Choose one of your ideas and write a poem.

- Firstly jot down some words to describe your monster like this:
  Icicle Monster – spiky hair, sharp teeth, bony fingers, glittering eyes, a cold stare.

- Think about what your monster would be doing. Look at the poem to help you: nibbling, munching, slurping, licking.

- Try putting your poem together. Here's the beginning of 'The Icicle Monster':
  Sharp teeth, spiky hair.
  Glittering eyes, a cold stare.
  Crunch, crackle, snicker, snackle,
  The icicle monster lives in there.
  Bony fingers …

The Dictionary

- When is a dictionary used?
  1. To find the correct meaning of a word.
  2. To find another way of saying a word.
  3. To find the correct spelling of a word.
- All the words are listed in alphabetical order. This means that they are listed in the order of the letters of the alphabet.

 A **Look at these words.**

---

wood *noun*
  1. A **wood** is a lot of trees, growing in one place.
  2. **Wood** is the trunk and branches of trees cut up and used to make things.
wool *noun*
  1. **Wool** is the hair of sheep and goats.
  2. **Wool** is the long fibres that are spun from the hair of sheep and goats.
worker *noun* **workers**
  A **worker** is person who works for a living.
workshop *noun* **workshops**
  A **workshop** is a place where things are mended.
world *noun*
  The **world** is the Earth and everything in it.
worm *noun* **worms**
  A **worm** is a long, thin animal that moves by wriggling its body along. Earthworms live in the soil.
wound¹ *noun* **wounds**
  A **wound** is an injury or a cut.
wound² *verb* **wounds, wounding, wounded**
  To **wound** someone is to injure or harm them.

wrap *verb* **wraps, wrapping, wrapped**
  To **wrap** is to cover something completely, such as a parcel.
wreath *noun* **wreaths**
  A **wreath** is an arrangement of flowers in a circle.
wreck¹ *noun* **wrecks**
  A **wreck** is a ship or building that has been badly damaged.
wreck² *verb* **wrecks, wrecking, wrecked**
  To **wreck** something is to damage it so badly that it cannot be used again.
wrestle *verb* **wrestles, wrestling, wrestled**
  To **wrestle** is to fight using the body as a weapon.
wretched *adjective*
  Wretched is very miserable or sad: *she felt wretched because she forgot Tony's birthday.*
wriggle *verb* **wriggles, wriggling, wriggled**
  If you **wriggle** you twist and turn your body around.
wrist *noun* **wrists**
  Your **wrist** is the joint between your arm and your hand.

---

1. Find the correct meanings of the words 'wriggle', 'wrist', 'wreath', 'world', 'wool' and 'wrap'.

2. Write each of the words in a sentence of your own.

3. The words 'wood' and 'wreck' have more than one meaning. Write a sentence for each word which shows their different meanings.

4. Write in alphabetical order the names of your friends (forenames or surnames), a list of 10 sports and 15 countries of the world.

Abracadabra!

The word 'magic' comes from the Greek word *magus* meaning a wise man. 'Magic' is also a word used to describe the tricks practised by conjurors and magicians to entertain their audiences. It has been practised since early times.

In some African tribes there are 'witch doctors' who 'make' magic to treat illness or to bring rain or a good harvest. A witch doctor is feared because he is usually the only person in the tribe to know the spells. These spells cast by witch doctors often have an effect, probably because the tribespeople believe in his power.

Certain spells in sentences or in single words may be recited to bring about magic. They are handed down from generation to generation with directions to repeat them absolutely word-for-word. If the magic doesn't work, it is said that a mistake has been made in the spell.

Sometimes objects are important in a spell but words are more so. In the story of 'Ali Baba and the Forty Thieves', for example, Ali Baba's brother couldn't get out of the thieves' cave because he had forgotten the words 'open sesame', which made the cave door open.

In many old stories such as 'Snow White and the Seven Dwarfs', 'Aladdin', the fairy tales of the Brothers Grimm and the stories of King Arthur, there is a witch or a wizard who has power over other people, sometimes for evil and sometimes for good.

Modern magic has come down to us from the street entertainers of the Middle Ages. They performed in castles for the kings and nobles and they entertained people at fairs and in market places. Usually they travelled with other performers. The troupe might include jugglers, tumblers, performing animals, actors, minstrels and clowns, much like those who would perform in a circus nowadays.

The best known magic word is probably 'abracadabra', which was originally Latin and was thought to cure illnesses such as fevers. It is often used with conjuring tricks where the magician pretends to do the impossible. A conjuror's most common trick is to make objects seem to appear from nowhere and then to disappear.

A **Answer these questions.**

1. Explain the origin of the word 'magic' and what it means.
2. What kinds of 'magic' does a witch doctor perform?
3. Why is a witch doctor feared?
4. What things are important for a spell to work?
5. Can you name stories or films where magical things happen, or stories which feature witches or wizards? Make a list of them.
6. What variety of performers would you find in a 'troupe'?
7. Where might these performers entertain their audiences nowadays?
8. What is the best known 'magic' word?
9. What is its origin?
10. What is a magician's most common trick?
11. Find out and list some tricks that conjurors practise on stage.

B **Anagramabra!**

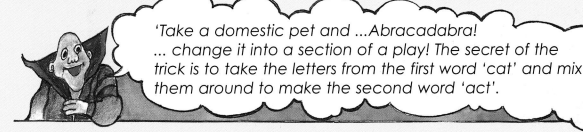

'Take a domestic pet and ...Abracadabra!
... change it into a section of a play! The secret of the
trick is to take the letters from the first word 'cat' and mix
them around to make the second word 'act'.

Try these:
1. Change a group of fighting men into a girl's name. *(4 letters)*
2. Change a direction into something sharp and pointed. *(5 letters)*
3. Change one of the five things on your hand into the hair which hangs over your forehead. *(6 letters)*
4. Turn an old weapon into things that you say. *(5 letters)*
5. Change an object used to tidy your hair into a garden plant. *(5 letters)*
6. Turn a part of a poem into 'help' or 'work'. *(5 letters)*
7. Turn large vehicles which transport loads into being slapped hard. *(6 letters)*
8. Turn 'not early' into a fairy story. *(4 letters)*
9. Turn our planet into something which beats inside your body. *(5 letters)*
10. Turn a low price into a fruit. *(5 letters)*
11. Turn all the land by the sea into a stable-animal. *(5 letters)*
12. Turn a soldier's walk into an ornament worn on a chain or bracelet. *(5 letters)*

Verb Tenses (1)

● Time is another word for tense. Actions occur at different times. Study this chart.

Verb (base word)	Present tense	Past tense	Future tense
To walk	I walk	I walked	I will walk
To swim	She swims	She swam	She will swim
To cram	We cram	We crammed	We will cram

 A Copy and complete this table.

Present tense	Past tense	Future tense
He knocks		
	They bought	
		It will begin
You eat		
		She will drink
I drop		
		We will forget

 B Rewrite this passage in both past and present tenses.

Helen will go home from school at three o'clock. She will meet her neighbours outside the house. Her younger brothers will be playing in the living-room. They will pay little attention to her as, instead, they will proceed to climb over all the furniture.

She will laugh and move into the kitchen where the dog will immediately scamper under the table. It will hide there and Helen will notice the apple pie on the floor. The dog will hear her shriek and will try to cover its ears. The boys will run into the kitchen and discover the mess. Their dad will blame them of course, when he will return. They will sweep it up and he will warn them about their future conduct.

 C Copy and complete the table below.

Verbs agree with nouns in singular and plural, e.g. The bird sings. The birds sing.

Singular	Plural
The horse runs	
	The spectators cheer
The summer was warm	
	The babies cry

Singular and Plural (1)

- Singular means only one. Plural means more than one.
  For many words, just add 's' to make a plural,
  e.g.   magician – magicians   conjuror – conjurors   spell – spells

  There are, however, many tricks to this rule. Here are some of them.
- For words ending with -ch, -sh, -s, -x, -z, add -es,
  e.g.   witch – witches, wish – wishes.
- For words ending with -f or -fe, add -s or change the -f to -ves,
  e.g.   thief – thieves.
- For words ending with a consonant followed by -y, change the -y to -ies,
  e.g. lady – ladies.
- For words ending in -o, add -s or -es,
  e.g.   piano – pianos, potato – potatoes.
- For some words, change the inside of the word,
  e.g.   man – men, tooth – teeth.
- Some words have no plural at all! e.g. pliers, trousers, scissors.

 A **Use the tricks to help you change these singular words into plurals.**

1. picture	**8.** dwarf	**15.** tomato
2. school	**9.** family	**16.** calf
3. volcano	**10.** floor	**17.** cuckoo
4. thief	**11.** direction	**18.** monkey
5. brother	**12.** woman	**19.** goose
6. hero	**13.** box	**20.** branch
7. half	**14.** boss	**21.** brush

B **Change the underlined words to plurals in the sentences below.**

1. The <u>witch doctor</u> cast the powerful <u>spell</u> in front of the <u>tribe</u>.
2. The <u>conjuror</u> performed the fantastic <u>trick</u>.
3. The <u>object</u> and the <u>word is</u> important in the <u>spell</u>.
4. The <u>magician</u> entertained the <u>audience</u> at the <u>circus</u>.
5. The <u>class</u> found <u>a shell</u> at the <u>beach</u>.
6. The <u>cook</u> prepared the <u>fish</u> in the <u>kitchen</u>.
7. The <u>thief</u> used <u>pliers</u> to prise open the <u>window</u>.
8. The <u>fairy</u> said the <u>lady</u> had to make <u>a wish</u>.

Suffixes (1) – Changing Nouns and Adjectives to Verbs

- We can add suffixes (word endings) to words to make new ones.
  Sometimes when we do this we change a noun or an adjective into a verb.

  noun   **suffix**   **verb**
  class   +   ify   =   classify
  I went swimming with my class yesterday.
  His job was to classify the new gemstones into rubies, sapphires or emeralds.

- When you add a suffix the root word can lose or gain a letter like this:

  adjective   **suffix**   **verb**
  memory + ise = memorise

 A   **Write down what each word in bold is: a noun or an adjective.**

1. It was a **simple** job to mend the puncture in her tyre.
2. With **regular** practice he could become a brilliant tennis player.
3. Susie loved **Drama** because she enjoyed singing, dancing and running around.
4. Susie also liked **quiet** moments to read her own stories.

- Now add the correct suffixes to make verbs.

  Root Word   **Suffixes**

  simple, regular, Drama, quiet   ate, ify, en, ise

- Write a sentence to show the meaning of the verb.

 B   **These verbs are harder. Match them to their meanings. Write down the number and the letter.**

1. advertise   2. deaden   3. investigate   4. locate

a) to find out the exact place of something or somewhere
b) to make well known or encourage selling
c) to make something dull and lifeless
d) to try to discover what has happened

 C   **Can you guess the meanings of these words? Check them in a dictionary.**

justify   fluctuate   eradicate

Verb Tenses (2)

- A verb is an action word, e.g. John walks. Anne talked. The bird sang.
- All verbs have a tense, which tells us the time of the action.

 Copy and complete this table.

Present tense	Past tense	Future tense
1. I write	I wrote	I will write
2. I take		
3. I steal		
4. I hide		
5. I ring		
6. I choose		
7. I bite		
8. I sing		
9. I stand		
10. I do		
11. I eat		
12. I swim		
13. I read		
14. I laugh		

B **Write as many verbs as you can think of in connection with actions involving 'speed', e.g. galloping, and 'talk' e.g. whispering.**

running ...

 Rewrite this paragraph. Choose suitable verbs to complete it.

I got a terrible fright the other day when I _____ into my bedroom and _____ two bats, real live bats! I nearly _____ with the shock. There they were, _____ to the curtain. I _____ down the stairs and immediately _____ my friend, Lisa, who recently joined a Bat Club, believe it or not. She _____ at my house within ten minutes. "Don't _____, they're lovely little creatures," she _____ me. Then she _____ the room, _____ over to the curtains and _____ the two little monsters. "Ah, look at them, Joan, aren't they cute?" _____ Lisa. "They're baby pipistrelles, fast asleep."

The Great Wheatcake

The word 'pyramid' is the Greek word for a wheatcake. The name was probably given by visiting Greek traders as a joke. The pyramid was thought of as a 'staircase to heaven', laid for the ruler. The largest of these is the 'Great Pyramid of the Pharaoh'. When built, the pyramid's four corners pointed exactly north, south, east and west. Deep inside it was a small room or chamber in which was placed the dead person's mummified body, together with jewels and other precious treasures.

Mummies are bodies embalmed to preserve them, wrapped with linen bandages and put into brightly painted caskets. It was thought that the king's soul would some day return to the body and occupy it again. All that might be needed in the afterworld was put into the tomb, including food and drink. On the walls were paintings and inscriptions telling the king how to avoid any dangers he might meet on the way back to life. The casket was placed inside a carved stone coffin called a sarcophagus. Sometimes this was in the rough shape of a person.

Over the centuries, robbers have broken into the pyramids and stolen the treasures. Some mummies were destroyed but many can still be seen in museums, especially in Egypt's capital city, Cairo. Some museums have mummified cats. Cats were sacred animals to the Egyptians.

Sometimes it is said that a curse will fall on anyone who disturbs a tomb or a pyramid. This may or may not be true, but it is strange the way some people have died mysteriously after opening pyramid-tombs to study them. The most famous is the sudden death of Lord Carnarvon, soon after he and Howard Carter discovered the tomb of Tutankhamun. His death was linked to the curse of Tutankhamun.

The statue of the sphinx beside the Great Pyramid has the body of a crouching lion and the head of a human. In mythology, the sphinx was a terrifying winged monster who devoured anyone who failed to answer her riddle: 'What is it that has one voice, four feet, then two feet, then finally three feet?'

Only the Greek Oedipus gave the correct answer and caused the creature's death: 'Man. He crawls as a baby, walks as an adult and leans on a stick when old.'

A   Answer these questions.

1. What is the Greek word for wheatcake?
2. Which is the largest of the pyramids? What is it like?
3. What is a 'mummy'?
4. What was placed in the tomb and what were on the walls?
5. What animal was sacred to the Egyptians?
6. What is a 'curse'? Check in a dictionary.
7. Describe the statue of the sphinx.

B   How can you tell the account 'The Great Wheatcake' is different from a story? Think about:

- how a story might begin, build-up and end
- whether it would be fact or fiction
- how it might describe things.

C   Read 'The Great Wheatcake' again.

1. Read the first sentence in paragraph four. Is this fact, fiction or an opinion? Write down your answer and say why.
2. Imagine you have disturbed a tomb. Tell the story of the curse that affected you.
- Describe where it takes place.
- Describe one or two characters (no more) who are different from each other.
- Think about how the story might begin, build-up and end.
  Make notes before you begin.

D   Try writing a pyramid poem.

It should have eight lines. The first should have one syllable, the second two and so on until the eighth and final line, which should have eight syllables. Read this one:

I

start at

the top of

Pyramid Hill

and headlong tumble

as fast as I can go

on my red green and yellow

mad - as - a - hatter toboggan

Mary Green

23

Confusing Words (2)

A **Write out these sentences inserting of/off into them.**

- 'of' means 'belonging to', 'coming from something' or 'made from'.
- 'off' means 'away', 'at a distance' or 'to a distance'.

1. The pyramid was thought _____ as a 'staircase to heaven'.
2. The coffin was made _____ stone and carved into the rough shape _____ a person.
3. The referee ordered the player _____ the field at the end _____ the game.
4. Hundreds _____ them floated _____ down the river.
5. The fox ran _____ with two _____ mother's hens.
6. Angela turned _____ the television before going _____ to bed.
7. Tim, the baby _____ the family, was afraid _____ the dog next door.
8. The sphinx had the body _____ a lion and the head _____ a human.
9. The tall runner set _____ before the rest _____ the field.
10. Which _____ you tore _____ the new cover _____ my book?

B **Write out these sentences inserting there/their/they're into them.**

- 'There' means 'in that place'.
- 'Their' means 'belonging to them'.
- 'They're' means 'they are'.

1. I went _____ yesterday.
2. They went _____ with _____ father.
3. _____ putting _____ books in _____ bags.
4. _____ will be a circus in town next week.
5. Are _____ any sweets left in the bag?
6. Scientists came to the valley to study _____ customs.
7. _____ never going _____ again.
8. Some birds obtain _____ food by digging with _____ bills.
9. _____ were hundreds of crows flying home to _____ nests in the wood.
10. _____ have been many visitors to Egypt over the years.
11. _____ stand the Pyramids. _____ still the main tourist attraction of Egypt.

Alphabetical Order

● Words are organised into alphabetical order in a dictionary.
As dictionaries become bigger they have more words beginning with the same letter or group of letters.

So, how do you find the word you want?

 Choose six names of people you know as a starting point.

1. The names should start with a different letter. Include members of your family and pets if you wish. Put the names into alphabetical order like this: Angus, Bob, Lennie, Mary, Rory, Zelda.

2. Now add one more name which starts with the same letter as one of those in your list like this: Meena.
Place it in the correct order.
Angus, Bob, Lennie, Mary, **Meena**, Rory, Zelda

'Mary' comes before 'Meena' because the second letter is 'a' in Mary and in the alphabet this comes before the 'e' in Meena.

3. Add another name to your list. This time the first two letters should be the same, like this: Angus, Bob, Lennie, **Mandy**, Mary, Meena, Rory, Zelda
'Mandy' comes before 'Mary' because the third letter 'n' comes before 'r'.

4. On your own add another name to your list in which the first three letters are the same. Place it in the correct order.

 Put these words into the correct alphabetical order.

story   poem   chant   rhythm   chorus   verse   character   setting   rhyme
magic   spell   syllable

 Use a dictionary to find these words. Which will you find first? Check the meanings.

accomplice   abuse   Aborigine   abattoir   abolition

Choose some words in your dictionary for a partner to find. Include words in which the first three letters are the same.

The Homecoming

Egil followed it, shouting. He had no idea that a pig could run so quickly. He saw it dash past some women who were washing clothes on the quay. Then it disappeared from sight.

He saw a Swedish boat as he raced around the corner. The owner, to judge from the number of his silver arm rings, was a very rich man. Slowly, the man turned round to face him. It was his father, home at last! The pig was nowhere to be found but that didn't matter. Egil greeted his father joyfully. He had so many questions to ask! Father explained that cousin Thorkild was bringing their old boat home. They had bought the new Swedish boat because they had so many treasures to carry home. He ordered his men to finish unloading the boat, while he and Egil set off for the farm.

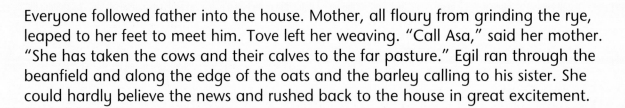

Egil ran to open the gate. The *thrall who was cleaning out the byre yelled in amazement as the cart trundled in. Gunnar was in the forge mending tools; the second thrall was lighting the fire in the bakehouse. They both ran out at the noise.

Everyone followed father into the house. Mother, all floury from grinding the rye, leaped to her feet to meet him. Tove left her weaving. "Call Asa," said her mother. "She has taken the cows and their calves to the far pasture." Egil ran through the beanfield and along the edge of the oats and the barley calling to his sister. She could hardly believe the news and rushed back to the house in great excitement.

Father spread out gifts for everyone. There were silver drinking cups and sweet-smelling spices for the whole family to enjoy. He gave lengths of silk cloth and silver neckbands to mother and the girls.

For Gunnar, there was a sword and to Egil he gave a silver charm and a beautiful knife. They all gasped with pleasure and thanked father. How wonderful it was to have him home again.

"Tonight we will sacrifice an ox," said mother, "and set it outside the door to thank the God Thor for father's safe return."

* Thrall – slave   *Giovanni Caselli*

A **Answer these questions.**

1. What was Egil chasing?
2. Why was he surprised?
3. What were slaves called and what jobs did they do?
4. Name all Egil's relatives.
5. How would the family celebrate Egil's father's return?
6. What does the story tell us about Viking life?

 B **Where is the setting of the story? Look for details in the story and write them down as notes, like this:**

The Setting of The Homecoming

1. near the sea in Sweden.
2. ...

How I Know

Egil sees his father's Swedish boat.

 C **Write a character sketch of Egil's father.**

First, look through the story and make notes like this:

Egil's Father

**What He Does and
What He Is Like**

1. A sailor and a farmer.

How I Know

He has returned from sea.
His family live on a farm.

Make four more points. Think about what his personality is like.
Now use your notes to write a character sketch. Write a paragraph.

Words with Double Consonants

● When two of the same consonants stand between two vowels, we break the word between the consonants.

let-ter   mir-ror

 Practise saying these words.

hol-low, stop-per, mut-ton, hic-cup, mug-ger, rob-ber, sud-den, nar-row, ter-ror, hor-ror, fit-ter, sul-len.

 Match the syllables in Sack A with those in Sack B and form 12 words.

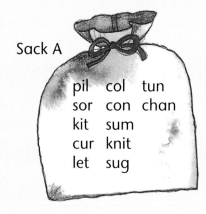

Sack A

pil	col	tun
sor	con	chan
kit	sum	
cur	knit	
let	sug	

Sack B

nect	low
rant	gest
ten	row
nel	tuce
nel	mer
ter	lect

C **Complete these words.**

1. marionette	_ _ pp _ _		**9.** sheep-meat	_ _ tt _ _
2. season	_ _ mm _ _		**10.** baby cat	_ _ tt _ _
3. raisin	_ _ rr _ _ _		**11.** yell or shout	_ _ ll _ _
4. fear	_ _ rr _ _		**12.** vegetable	_ _ bb _ _ _
5. tube	_ _ nn _ _		**13.** colour	_ _ ll _ _
6. small town	_ _ ll _ _ _		**14.** eraser	_ _ bb _ _
7. condiment	_ _ pp _ _		**15.** thief	_ _ bb _ _
8. looking glass	_ _ rr _ _		**16.** not sweet	_ _ tt _ _

 Make sentences using these words.

quarrel collect butter shallow sudden dessert arrow swimmer

28

Adverbs

● Adverbs are words which tell us more about a verb.

e.g. (a) Egil had no idea that pigs could run so quickly.

(b) He greeted his father joyfully.

(c) Asa and Tove got beautifully decorated neckbands from their father.

 A **Copy the sentences below. Insert suitable adverbs from the list.**

expertly slowly clearly excitedly peacefully gladly
bitterly safely fiercely sadly lawfully cowardly

1. Egil could see the ships _____ from the town.

2. Now people could sleep _____ without fear of attack from raiders.

3. Gunnar, his brother, could handle the plough _____ .

4. _____ , the man turned round to face him.

5. Everyone followed father _____ into the house.

6. Six new calves had been born _____ in the spring.

7. The winters along the Baltic Lands were _____ cold.

8. The family went home _____ after Thorkild's funeral.

9. "If we find Tostig here, we may _____ kill him."

10. Wild tribes were lying in wait for us, and attacked us _____ .

11. The manner of Thorkild's killing was _____ and vile.

12. Egil agreed _____ to go to the King's Hall.

 B **If the adjective in a sentence ends in '-y', you must change the '-y' to '-ily' to form the adverb.**

e.g. merry – merrily, angry – angrily.

Make these words into adverbs and put each one into a sentence.

lazy, happy, heavy, hasty, noisy, wary, easy, lucky.

 **C** **Using the ideas from the sentences in A, write a story about Thorkild's killing.**

Use as many adverbs as you can.

Word Building

- Many words which have the same letter patterns are also linked by meaning. Both these things can help us remember the spelling.

medical   **medicine**

I had a medical examination to check I was well again.
The medicine I took for my illness made me feel better.

- Remember to note where the spelling changes, too.

 Pair these words.

number	circuit	competitors	geography
competition	geology	circle	numerous

B **Use the words in A to complete these sentences.**

1. When we learn about _____ in my class we always use the large globe.
2. The game meant that we had to move in a _____ round our partners.
3. There were _____ ants moving backwards and forwards, carrying all sorts of tiny things.
4. His rainforest painting with its bright colours and sweeping brushwork won first prize in the _____ .
5. "Can all the _____ line up at the starting post, please!" shouted my teacher.
6. She made an electrical _____ during Science and was pleased with the result.
7. "_____ nine, right on time !" laughed the magician as he pulled nine roses out of his pocket.
8. We went to the _____ museum last week to see the rocks and minerals.

 Use your dictionary and find a word with the same letter pattern and a similar meaning to match each of these:

bicycle   business   mysterious   opposite

Can you think of any other words which match? Check again in the dictionary.

Using Commas Carefully

- Commas can separate different parts of a sentence from each other.
  When we use commas correctly, they help us to read with expression and understand more easily what we are reading.

 The following sentences have either too many commas or not enough. Read them first, then write them out putting the commas in suitable places.

1. Kelly gobbled down her breakfast put on her coat grabbed her bag, ran down the road and managed to get to school two minutes before the bell went.

2. "If I've told you once I've told you a million times not to leave your toys all over the floor," sighed Kelly's mother.

3. Kelly, was given, a bar of chocolate, a book mark, and a pencil, because her story was so well written.

4. Kelly's little cat, Threepence, is a tough little cat, with a broken tooth, and a tattered ear.

5. Leroy Kelly's friend lives next door.

6. Kelly's favourite book which was written by Lewis Carroll is called *Alice's Adventures In Wonderland*.

 Write a story choosing from one of these titles. Organise your story into a beginning, middle and end. You will need to write at least three paragraphs.

1. The Tiger Who Always Smiled   2. Crash! Bang! Wallop!
3. Leroy's Favourite Things   4. Bones, Bones, Bones
5. The Acrobats   6. Kelly's Special Day Out

Use commas where you need to.

When you have finished, read your work through with expression, checking that the commas are in the right place. Make any changes you need to.

Suffixes (2)

● A suffix is a syllable added to the end of a word to form a new word.
E.g: speech**less**, judge**ment**, wonder**ful**.

 Form new words by adding -less to each of the following.

match	sun	tooth	taste	luck
grace	hope	end	care	point

 Match the following adjectives with one of the nouns.

cloudless	sea	painless	astronaut
bottomless	task	goalless	driver
homeless	athlete	weightless	painting
tireless	sky	reckless	draw
thankless	tramp	priceless	injection

 Form new words by adding -ness to each of the following.

rude	sudden	kind	humble	gracious
awful	careless	speechless	hopeless	

 Add -ness or -less to the following words.

Rule: If a word ends in -y (e.g. happy), we change it to an -i when adding the suffix (e.g. happiness).

ugly	pity	dizzy	giddy	ready
pretty	silly	mercy	penny	

 The following words contain some commonly used suffixes. Divide them into their syllables.

corporation   cor – por – a – tion
politician
merriment
Protestantism
unbelievable

Suffixes (3)

 A **-ARY, -ERY or -ORY?** **Select the correct suffix to complete the word.**

Janu	flatt	myst
mem	cemet	tempor
ordin	territ	compuls
jewell	volunt	laborat
machin	annivers	cel
tribut	element	categ

B **-ANCE OR -ENCE?** **Select the correct suffix to complete the word.**

rom	signific	experi
interfer	entr	viol
nuis	turbul	pati
excell	magnific	assist
arrog	ambul	obedi

C **Give two examples of each suffix.**

-IC	-HOOD	-MENT
-DOM	-FORM	-ION

D **-OUS OR -IOUS?** **Try to identify the words below.**

very well known	_ _ _ ous	meat-eating	_ _ _ _ _ _ _ _ _ous
huge	_ _ _ _ _ ous	dangerous	p _ _ _ _ ous
extremely valuable	_ _ _ _ ious	kind	_ _ _ _ _ ous
amazing	s _ _ _ _ _ _ ous	jealous	_ _ _ ious
devoted to reading	s _ _ ious	aware of	c _ _ _ ious
of different kinds	_ _ _ ious	inquisitive	_ _ ious
grave	_ _ _ ious	shining	l _ _ _ _ ous
worried	_ _ _ ious	will betray	t _ _ _ _ _ _ ous

Professor Branestawm's Letters

"I'm going to write some letters for half an hour and I'm not to be disturbed," said the professor to his housekeeper, arranging his five pairs of glasses nice and neatly on his forehead for when he wanted to use them, "and I'll have a cup of tea when I've finished." "Yes, sir," said Mrs Flittersnoop, and she went to the kitchen to finish reading her book.

The clock on the mantelpiece said four o'clock as the professor fastened the safety pins that he had on his coat because the buttons had fallen off, and sat down to write. His pen was simply old and ancient because he'd forgotten to change the nib and it was going scratch, scratch, squeak as it went over the paper.

He wrote to his auntie and his cousin and his special friend. He wrote to the butcher by mistake about some cabbages and he wrote to the local coal people to say that the coal they had sent was all dirty. He wrote to the mayor about a nasty smell that seemed as if it might be drains but was really a disused bone that Mrs Flittersnoop's sister's dog had pushed under the carpet. Then he wrote to the B.B.C. to say that someone was making squeaky noises on the wireless and to the laundry to ask if they would send back two buttons that were missing from his blue shirt.

The professor then took an envelope and addressed it to his friend Colonel Dedshott of the Catapult Cavaliers, who lived in Shoobangfire Cottage, Missfire Lane in the town of Great Pagwell.

He looked at the clock through his long-sighted spectacles and he was just wondering what to write next when Mrs Flittersnoop tapped at the door and came in with a cup of tea and a nice big piece of coconut cake.

R.W. Heath

Answer these questions.

1. At what time did Professor Branestawm expect to finish his letters?
2. How many letters did he write?
3. What was odd about the letter he wrote to the butcher?
4. What was odd about the letter he wrote to the local coal people?
5. What was silly about the letters he wrote to the laundry and the B.B.C?
6. What do you think is interesting about Colonel Dedshott's name and address?

 Write a character sketch of Professor Branestawm.

First, look through the story and make notes like this:

What He Is Like   **How I Know**
He has odd habits.   He wears five pairs of glasses.

Make as many points as you can. Think about what he looks like and what his personality is like. Think about his name.

Now use your notes to write the character sketch.

 What do you think Professor Branestawm's home is like?

Look for clues in the passage and make notes like this:

Professor Branestawm's Home
What It Is Like   **How I Know**

Write two paragraphs about Professor Branestawm's home.
Use your notes to write the first paragraph.
The second paragraph should add more information. You should say what else it could be like, given Professor Branestawm's character.

 Find as many funny names as you can in the passage and write down what they tell you about each character or place.

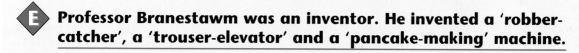 **Professor Branestawm was an inventor. He invented a 'robber-catcher', a 'trouser-elevator' and a 'pancake-making' machine.**

Invent some things of your own.

Writing a Letter

A **Read this letter carefully.**

> **1** *Whateveritis Cottage*
> *Thingummy Lane*
> *Great Pagwell*
> *AB1 2XY*
> *24th September*
>
> **2** *Dear Dedshott*
>
> **3** *Come and see me tomorrow if you can. I have an invention that will change all our ideas of travel. It looks something like a cross between a typewriter, an egg-timer and a conjuring trick, but you mustn't let appearances deceive you. I'm eager to demonstrate my new machine, so until I see you.*
>
> **4** *Your good friend*
>
> *Professor Branestawm*

Important Points

1 The writer's address is written at the top of the right-hand side of the page. The date is written under the last line of the address.

2 The greeting uses capital letters.

3 Some letters have paragraphs.

4 The ending is written on the left-hand side and the writer's name is placed below it. (Yours faithfully, Yours sincerely, Best wishes, Yours ...)

B **Professor Branestawm would address the envelope to Colonel Dedshott like this.**

> *Colonel Dedshott*
> *Shoobangfire Cottage*
> *Missfire Lane*
> *AB1 2PQ*
> *Great Pagwell*

Note the use of capital letters.

1. Draw an envelope and write your address properly on it.

2. Write out this letter correctly.

22 Strand Road, Preston, Lancashire, PR1 2TS. 12th June. Dear Aunt Brenda, It was very kind of you to send me the money for my birthday. I was delighted as I have been saving for a new bike since Easter. We are all looking forward to seeing both you and Uncle Mike when you visit us next month. Lots of love, Carol.

A Letter To ...

● Look back to the previous page to remind yourself about the layout of a letter.

 Write Colonel Dedshott's reply to Professor Branestawm's invitation.

(a) It should thank him for the invitation.

(b) It should accept the invitation. You are delighted...

(c) Indicate that you are looking forward to an interesting afternoon.

 From the passage 'Profesor Branestawm's Letters' on page 34, choose one of the letters that the professor wrote.

Write out that letter as you think he would have written it.

 **Write a letter to a famous person.**

Write a draft letter to someone you admire, maybe a footballer, an athlete, an actor or a pop singer. What could you ask this person? Do they like being famous?

What is their favourite television programme, food or animal?

How could you ask them for their autograph? Would you ask for a photograph?

Make a list of all the things you want to ask before you start.

 Write the reply.

Now write the reply from the person to whom you wrote your letter. Were they helpful? Did they send you an autograph?

Vesuvius, the Victor

Suddenly there was a terrific explosion and the ground shook violently. The children screamed and put their hands over their ears to shut out the horrendous noise. Their parents came rushing to find them, tied cushions on their heads, grabbed the children and, rushing to the door, ordered the slaves to follow them.

Red flames were leaping wildly across the sky. Clouds of thick smoke engulfed the summit of Vesuvius and rocks were being hurled out of its crater. Vesuvius the volcano was erupting.

Hot streams of lava slid down the mountain slope and were fast approaching the town. Pumice fell like massive hailstones from the sky, pelting people and rattling on cobblestones. Marcus and Julius were protected from the falling stones by the cushions on their heads.

Terrified people were running in every direction, but some refused to leave their houses, feeling safer inside.

It was getting darker and darker. Soon the only light was from the fierce flames and red rocks which lit the sky like shooting stars. Birds were falling dead in the streets, overcome by poisonous fumes.

The children, who were already breathless from running, spluttered and coughed with the choking gases. The air was heavy, black and stifling. Would they ever escape?

They ran and ran, heading towards the city gates. Crowds of people were already there, trying to get out. Poor Marcus and Julius were pushed about as panic-stricken people jostled for an escape route.

At last they stood on the far side of the city wall and ran again, to leave the threatened Pompeii far behind.

There would be no gladiator fights at Pompeii's amphitheatre now; it lay buried in smouldering black ash.

The volcano had conquered a whole town. Vesuvius was the mighty, proud and cruel victor.

Sue Peasgood

Answer these questions.

1. What is Vesuvius? Describe what was happening to it.
2. How do you know the Romans had slaves?
3. How were Marcus and Julius protected from the falling stones?
4. What happened to the birds?
5. Where would the children find their escape?
6. What did they find when they reached the city gates?
7. What do you think gladiator fights are? Why would there be no more?
8. Why was Vesuvius called 'the victor'?

 Here are some brief notes about how the people felt and what happened to them. Write a paragraph in your own words using the notes. Give the paragraph a heading.

1. The children screamed and put their hands over their ears to shut out the noise.
2. People were hit by pumice stone.
3. Some people felt safer in their houses and wouldn't leave.
4. The children were coughing, choking from the gases.
5. People were panic-stricken and terrified.

 Read paragraphs one, two and three again.

1. Use key words to select information about how the volcano was erupting and what was coming out of it. For example: explosion, ground shook, flames.
2. Now use the information to draw a diagram of Vesuvius erupting and label it.

 Find out more about Vesuvius and Pompeii.

You will need to look in the library or use ICT. Choose information and in your own words write two paragraphs under two headings.

 Write your own disaster story.

Think of some other things that have caused disasters, such as hurricanes, fog and earthquakes. Write a story about a character who is faced with a disaster. Remember to describe the event in detail using adjectives and adverbs.

Book Review – Gathering Ideas

● Read a book of your own choice, e.g. from the class, school or local library, or a book from your own collection at home.

 Answer these questions to help you write your review of the book you have just chosen and read.

What is the title of the book?
Who is the author?
What do you know about the author?
Who are the main characters?
Where and when does the story take place?
What was the best part of the story?
What was the 'mood' of the story – happy, sad, adventurous?
What is your opinion of the book? Talk about the cover and any illustrations.
What about the words: too hard or too easy? Would you read it again?
How well do the cover and illustrations match the text?

Gender

- Nouns such as man and woman tell us whether we are talking about something which is male or female.

- Sometimes a noun may change. The female noun can have the ess suffix added.

  author   authoress

  We call this changing gender.

- However, most people no longer use certain words with ess, such as authoress. Female as well as male writers like to be called the same, to show they are equal. So both are called authors.

 A **Complete these crossword puzzles by writing down the correct gender.**

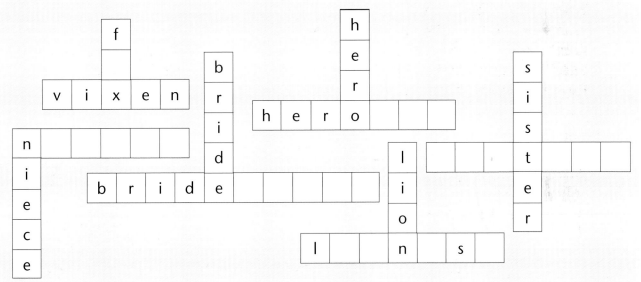

B **Write down the correct gender of these nouns:**

nun, husband, prince, duchess, empress, count, she, god, uncle, daughter, bull, boar.

C **Work out the male names for these female ones:**

Christina, Josephine, Claudine, Georgina, Paula, Alexandra.

D **Read the words below. Write down those most people don't use today. Then check what they mean:**

waitress, huntress, empress, poetess, spinster, hostess, stewardess, governess.
Of the ones we do use, decide when or where we use them.

Adjectives

- Adjectives are the words which are used to tell us more about nouns (people, places or things).

  e.g. Mr Pikelett was a small, skinny, old man with disgusting hands.
- The words small, skinny, old and disgusting are all adjectives.
- They tell us more about Mr Pikelett.

 Write out these sentences and circle the adjectives.

1. Roald Dahl's interesting, exciting and funny books are read by many boys and girls.
2. The graceful ballerina danced for the enthusiastic audience.
3. John scored two wonderful goals in the last minute.
4. The headteacher was an untidy, quiet little fellow with a big bald head.
5. The fast river flowed through the lush, green countryside.
6. Chocolate is a delicious and marvellous sweet.
7. The hungry thrush fed on a fat, juicy worm.
8. The shrubs in the big, green park are very ornamental.

 Think up suitable adjectives for the following nouns.

chocolate   sweet-shop   toffee   hands

 Copy this paragraph and underline the adjectives.

Large chocolate factories took their work very seriously. They had inventing rooms. I used to imagine a long white room like a huge laboratory with pots of chocolate and creamy fudge and all sorts of delicious fillings bubbling away. Men and women in white coats moved between the bubbling pots, tasting and mixing their wonderful new inventions. I used to imagine myself there, suddenly coming up with something so absolutely, unbearably delicious that I would grab it in my hand, rush out of the laboratory and along the corridor right into the office of the Great Mr Choco himself. "I've got it, Sir! It's fantastic! It's marvellous! It's fabulous! It's irresistible!"

Overused Words – Went/Then

1. The old man went along the road.

2. The old man hobbled slowly along the road.

The second sentence gives us a better idea of how an old man might walk.

A **Replace the word 'went' in these sentences with the more interesting words from the box.**

galloped marched trotted scampered hopped slid slithered
waddled crawled scurried cantered trundled skimmed rushed

1. The brave centurion (*went*) on in front of his army.

2. The athletic water skier (*went*) smoothly across the water's surface.

3. The beautiful stallion (*went*) swiftly over the fence.

4. The young foal (*went*) after the mare.

5. The squirrels (*went*) up to their drey in the trees.

6. The horse (*went*) along beside the jockey.

7. The duck (*went*) into the water and swam off to its mate.

8. Hot streams of lava (*went*) down the mountain slope.

9. The slimy snake hissed and (*went*) away.

10. The donkey and cart (*went*) down the dusty track.

● Sometimes we overuse the word 'then'. Read this passage:
Then there was a huge explosion. Then the ground shook. Then the children screamed. Then they put their hands over their ears and then their parents came rushing along.

B **Copy the paragraph and replace 'then' with words from the box.**

at midday shortly afterwards suddenly eventually soon
while unfortunately almost immediately straight away

Caius came to collect the boys from school. (*Then*) they wandered back home through the bustling streets. (*Then*) Marcus began kicking a stone along the ruts worn away by the carts that trundled along the roads after sunset. (*Then*) they reached the crossroads. Caius stopped to chat with friends who collect water at the fountain. (*Then*) they waited, Marcus and Julius peered into the shops. (*Then*) the shopkeepers were beginning to prepare for the midday rest. (*Then*) they closed the great wooden shutters. Caius crossed the street and (*then*) Marcus and Julius followed him home.

Looking for Clues

A detective is a police officer whose job is to investigate crimes and catch the culprits. There are also private detectives who are hired to carry out special investigations. They are not police officers.

Those in fiction tend to be private detectives. These types of stories became very popular in the nineteenth century. The most successful one of all was Sir Arthur Conan Doyle's Sherlock Holmes. This fictional private investigator set a pattern which most detectives in mystery stories have followed ever since.

The work of the real modern-day detective requires great skill and patience. He or she may have to work for months without finding any obvious clues. Nowadays, science can come to his or her aid, revealing clues invisible to the naked eye. However, much of the detective's work still consists of asking questions.

Let's imagine a typical serious crime.

A dead man has been found in London, England, with clear signs that he has been murdered. There are no fingerprints or evidence which gives any clue to the murderer except a very old and dirty cap of unusually large size beside the body. The dust from the lining of the cap shows, under the microscope, quantities of grains of flour. Nothing else is found. The only line of inquiry which suggests itself is to search at all bakeries, flour-warehouses and other places where flour is handled, for a man with a noticeably large head.

One day in a small bakery, a detective finds that a man named Harry Thomson, who worked there a few weeks earlier, left his job the day after the murder. Nothing is known of him except his address, but the manager remembers that he had a very large head. His landlady recalls him mentioning an unmarried sister who kept a vegetable stall in Scotland.

Without stopping inquiries in London, the search is continued in Scotland. A single woman named Johnstone who once owned a market stall is traced to a country village. She says she has a brother who is a baker, but that she has not seen him for several years. She says that it is true that he has a big head and gives his name as George Johnstone. She produces a small photograph of him taken three years earlier. The photograph is enlarged and sent out with a description of a baker named George Johnstone alias (also known as) Harry Thomson, aged 35, who is wanted for questioning. In a short time, Johnstone is found in Yorkshire working as a baker and is arrested.

Answer these questions.

1. What was the serious crime described in the passage?
2. What was the only line of inquiry which detectives could take?
3. What was Harry Thomson's real name?
4. Were the detectives successful with their inquiries? How do you know?
5. What do you think Harry Thomson was like? Choose from these words and write three sentences about him: clever, careless, friendly, dangerous, musical, married, deceitful.

 Use your dictionary to find the meanings of the following words.

investigate	culprits	private	popular
evidence	microscope	inquiry	alibi

 Fact or fiction?

1. 'A detective is a police officer whose job is to investigate crimes ... ' Is this fact or fiction?
2. Who was Sherlock Holmes? Was he fact or fiction? Explain why.
3. Is the case of Harry Thomson fact or fiction? Think carefully and explain why.

Make five points in note form which list the clues that led the police to arrest Harry Thomson. Number your points 1 to 5.

 Decide what sub-headings 'Looking for Clues' could have.

Think of four and write them down.

 Find out more about Sherlock Holmes.

1. Look in the library and use ICT. Choose three points and make notes.
2. Use the information from **C.2.** above and the notes you have made and write a paragraph about Sherlock Holmes. End your paragraph by saying why you think Sherlock Holmes was so popular.

Adventure in Egypt

 A **Write more words to describe when you feel afraid, trapped and safe.**

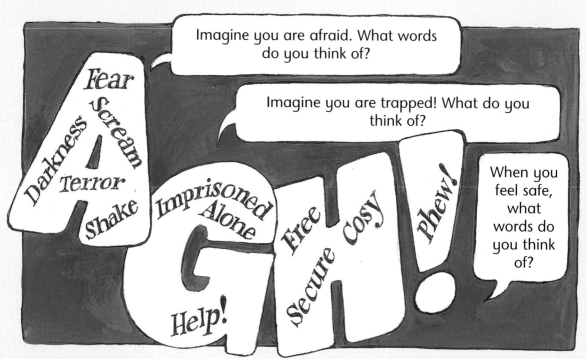

 B **Read the passage below.**

'It was unbelievable! Here we were, at long last, deep inside the famous Great Pyramid of Egypt. In the shadows cast by the lights from the entrance, we gazed in wonder at the curious inscriptions which had been carved into the stone walls of this incredible tomb so long ago. Suddenly, there was a loud resounding bang and we were plunged into darkness.'

How did you feel? What did you do? What supplies did you have – torches, food? What did you see? Did mummies come alive? Did a sarcophagus open? You had to rack your brains ... .

C **Write about what happened next.**

How did you all escape or were you rescued? Did an inscription hold any solution? Was there a riddle or a puzzle to solve in order to re-open the entrance to the tomb? Can you write out the riddle?

 D **Write about how you and your companions felt when the door to your freedom was opened.**

Would you ever visit Egypt again?

Adjectives and Nouns

 What are adjectives? Write a definition.

The house of a well-known business person has been burgled.

The police are currently trying to make photofits of the two possible suspects who may be involved. (Robber A and Robber B.)

Find adjectives that would help them to do this.

Robber A

Height _____ tall _____

Weight _____

Shape of face _____

Eyes _____

Nose _____

Clothes _____

 What are nouns? Write a definition.

Meanwhile an investigator attempts to list the stolen items (nouns) in his notebook. Help by copying the lists started below. Add your own stolen 'nouns' and use adjectives to describe them.

Stolen goods list		
number	**adjectives**	**nouns**
two	golden	necklace
one	portable	television
one	black	video

Robber B

Height _____

Weight _____

Shape of face _____

Eyes _____

Nose _____

Clothes _____

 Find the nouns and adjectives in this passage and list them under the headings: 'Nouns' and 'Adjectives'.

The policeman wouldn't tell them anything more and they climbed the stairs in silence. Aunt Martha opened the wooden door and took them into the cosy sitting-room. Grandma was awake now and sat up at once, full of curiosity. Emil and Pont stood by the round table, eager and expectant. "It's like this," said the policeman. "The scruffy thief who was tracked down this morning, thanks to Emil Tischbein, has been identified as the man who robbed a large bank in Hanover last month. We've been searching for him for some time now. He has made a full statement, and most of the money has been found sewn into the lining of his jacket – all in one hundred pound notes. A fortnight ago the bank offered a reward for his capture. You caught him," the policeman said to Emil with a meaningful nod, "so the reward is yours. The superintendent asked me to give you his kind regards and to tell you he is very glad to see courage and enterprise rewarded in this way."

Macavity – the Mystery Cat

Macavity's a Mystery Cat: he's called the Hidden Paw –
For he's the master criminal who can defy the Law.
He's the bafflement of Scotland Yard, the Flying Squad's
    despair:
For when they reach the scene of the crime – *Macavity's not
    there!*

Macavity, Macavity, there's no one like Macavity,
He's broken every human law, he breaks the law of gravity.
His powers of levitation would make a fakir stare,
And when you reach the scene of crime – *Macavity's not
    there!*
You may seek him in the basement, you may look up in
    the air –
But I tell you once and once again – *Macavity's not there!*

Macavity's a ginger cat, he's very tall and thin;
You would know him if you saw him, for his eyes are sunken
    in.
His brow is deeply lined with thought, his head is slightly
    domed;
His coat is dusty from neglect, his whiskers are uncombed.
He sways his head from side to side, with movements like a
    snake;
And when you think he's half asleep, he's always wide
    awake.

Macavity, Macavity, there's no one like Macavity,
For he's a fiend in feline shape, a monster of depravity.
You may meet him in a by-street, you may see him in the
    square –
But when a crime's discovered, then *Macavity's not there!*

He's outwardly respectable. (They say he cheats at cards.)
And his footprints are not found in any file of Scotland
    Yard's.
And when the larder's looted or the jewel-case is rifled,
Or when the milk is missing, or another Peke's been stifled,
Or the greenhouse glass is broken, and the trellis past
    repair –
Ay, there's the wonder of the thing! *Macavity's not there!!*

And when the Foreign Office find a Treaty's gone astray,
Or the Admiralty lose some plans and drawings by the way,
There may be a scrap of paper in the hall or on the
    stair –
But it's useless to investigate – Macavity's not there!
And when the loss has been disclosed, the Secret Service say:
'It must have been Macavity!' – but he's a mile away.
You'll be sure to find him resting, or a-licking of his thumbs,
Or engaged in doing complicated long division sums.

Macavity, Macavity, there's no one like Macavity,
There never was a Cat of such deceitfulness and suavity.
He always has an alibi, and one or two to spare:
And whatever time the deed took place – MACAVITY WASN'T
    THERE!
And they say that all the cats whose wicked deeds are widely
    Known
(I might mention Mungojerrie, I might mention Griddle-
    bone)
Are nothing more than agents for the cat who all the time
Just controls the operations: the Napoleon of Crime!

T.S. Eliot

 A Answer these questions.

1. Who is Macavity?

2. List some of Macavity's crimes.

3. Do you think his crimes are serious? Why?

4. List two of Macavity's 'alibis'.

5. What is your opinion of Macavity?

6. What does 'the Napoleon of Crime' mean?

 B Write your own cat verse.

If you can, think of a cat you know. First list adjectives to describe it.
Then try to work out a chorus.

 **C T.S. Eliot wrote many other cat poems in a
book called *Old Possum's Book of Practical Cats*.**

Find Mungojerrie and Rumpelteazer. In what way are they like Macavity? Read
The Song of the Jellicles, too.

Windy Day at the Market

In the town of Bunbridge, the shops were waking up. Doors were unlocked, shelves were restocked and counters were dusted and polished. Blank blinds were lifted, shutters were shifted and stalls were set out in the sun.

The wandering wind was trapped in the alleys and baffled by high brick walls. It rattled the lids of the clattering bins and shook all the ill-fitting gates. It howled around the houses, blew under the doors, moaned at the windows and sneaked up through the floors.

The little bus from Cobbler's Green rumbled along the High Street and stopped in Market Square. Mothers and aunties and grannies got off, clutching their shopping baskets. The wind went to meet them, twisting their skirts, tugging their scarf-ends, making them hold their hats.

Coming and going and to-ing and fro-ing, shoppers and stallholders moved in a crowding, cheerful confusion. P.C. Samuel Spindleberry, lean as a beanpole, stood in the doorway, keeping an eye on things.

Above the sound of the buying and selling, the good-humoured banter and shouting and yelling, could be heard the constant flap and slap of canvas. The restless wind was amusing itself with the hoods and skirts of the stalls.

A **Answer these questions.**

1. What was the name of the market town?
2. What time of day did the story take place? How do you know?
3. What was the weather like?
4. From where did the bus come?
5. Who got off the bus?
6. What special day was it in the market square?
7. What did P.C. Samuel Spindleberry do for a living? What does 'spindle' mean? Use your dictionary. What does the word tell you about him?
8. Why do you think he was 'keeping an eye on things'?

B **The passage is very descriptive about the weather. Find verbs (action words) which describe what the wind did.**

C **How did the people feel in Bunbridge – cross, happy, sad? Find words which tell you.**

If you were in Bunbridge on a windy day how would you feel?

D **P.C. Spindleberry was as 'lean as a beanpole'. This is called a simile because it is saying he is like or the same as a beanpole.**

1. Match the words in the box on the left to those on the right, e.g. a) red as beetroot

fit brave fresh slow		tortoise mule beetroot
busy mad slippery proud		bee fiddle lion hatter
green stubborn red		grass eel daisy peacock

2. Think of your own similes for these: the wind, Bunbridge, the bus, the shoppers. Look in the passage for ideas and write it out like this:

The wind was as ...

E **When you read it, the passage moves along as though it was a windy day. Some of the words rhyme: 'Doors were unlocked'/'shelves were restocked'.**

Find others. Use them along with some rhymes of your own to write a poem called 'The Wind' or think of your own title.

Paragraphs (1)

- A paragraph is a group or collection of sentences which describe one main idea or one piece of action.
- Paragraphs break a story into sections to make it more interesting.
- You often have 'opening', 'middle' and 'ending' paragraphs in a story.

 Look at the passage 'Windy Day at the Market' (page 50) and answer the following.

1. How many paragraphs do you see in the passage?
2. The first few words in each paragraph tell us something about the rest of the paragraph. Using the first few words, complete the following sentences.
   (a) The first paragraph tells us about ...
   (b) The second paragraph tells us about ...
   (c) The third paragraph tells us about ...
   (d) The fourth paragraph tells us about ...
   (e) The fifth paragraph tells us about ...

 Answer these questions.

1. Which paragraph do you think best fits the title of the passage? Why do you think that?
2. Think of another title for the passage.
3. Write out the paragraph that best suits your choice of title.

C Write a short paragraph describing the shopping activities of the women in the passage.

What stalls did they pass? What were the smells and sounds? What did they buy?

Nouns

- A noun is the name of a person, animal, place or thing.

  e.g. My name is **Hugo**.

  I live in **America**.

  I collect rare **stamps**.

  My pet **dinosaur** is long dead!

 Here are some 'noun-sacks'. Draw your own and fill them with collections of different nouns.

Countries — England

Clothes — Jeans

Animals — Dog

People — Teacher

Places — Airport

Cars — Jeep

Make three more 'noun-sacks'. Use your dictionary to help you.

 Copy the sentences and underline the nouns.

1. The magpie builds a roof over its nest in large bushes or trees.
2. Areena noticed an expensive stamp in her collection.
3. I received a letter from Lisa and a postcard from Brian.
4. On our hiking trip, we gathered leaves, cones and some conkers.
5. Drinking straws, autographs, matchbooks and menus are also possible collectables.
6. Favourites with collectors are model railways and model cars.
7. About two thousand years ago, Roman children played with model soldiers.
8. The waiter put the coffee, milk and sugar on the table.

Night Mail

I

This is the night mail crossing the border,
Bringing the cheque and the postal order.

Letters for the rich, letters for the poor,
The shop at the corner and the girl next
door.

Pulling up Beattock, a steady climb –
The gradient's against her, but she's on
time.

Past cotton grass and moorland boulder
Shovelling white steam over her shoulder,

Snorting noisily as she passes
Silent miles of wind-bent grasses.

Birds turn their heads as she approaches,
Stare from the bushes at her black-faced
coaches.

Sheep dogs cannot turn her course,
They slumber on with paws across.

In the farm she passes no one wakes,
But a jug in the bathroom gently shakes.

II

Dawn freshens, the climb is done,
Down towards Glasgow she descends.
Towards the steam tugs yelping down the
glade of cranes,
Towards the fields of apparatus, the
furnaces
Set on the dark plain like giant chessmen,
All Scotland waits for her:
In the dark glens, beside the pale-green
lochs
Men long for news.

III

Letters of thanks, letters from banks,
Letters of joy from girl and boy,
Receipted bills and invitations
To inspect new stock or visit relations
And applications for situations
And timid lovers' declarations
And gossip, gossip, from all the nations,
News circumstantial, news financial,
Letters with holiday snaps to enlarge in,
Letters with faces scrawled in the margin,
Letters from uncles, cousins and aunts,
Letters to Scotland from the South of
France,
Letters of condolence to Highlands and
Lowlands,
Notes from overseas to Hebrides –

Written on paper of every hue,
The pink, the violet, the white and the
blue,
The chatty, the catty, the boring,
adoring,
The cold and official and the heart
outpouring,
Clever, stupid, short and long,
The type and printed and the spelt all
wrong.

IV

Thousands are still asleep
Dreaming of terrifying monsters,
Or of friendly tea beside the band at
Cranston's or Crawford's,
Asleep in working Glasgow, asleep in well-
set Edinburgh,
Asleep in granite Aberdeen,
They continue their dreams;
And shall wake soon and long for letters,
And none will hear the postman's knock
Without a quickening of the heart,
For who can bear to feel himself
forgotten?

W.H. Auden

Answer these questions.

1. What is the 'night mail' – a car, a train or an aeroplane? When you've chosen say what type you think it is and why.
2. What does it carry? Give five examples.
3. What border does it cross?
4. List four of the places it passes.
5. Describe two of the places.
6. What kind of dreams do the people dream?
7. Why do they 'long for letters'?
8. Explain what you think is meant by the phrases 'News circumstantial', 'news financial', 'lovers' declarations'. Your dictionary may help you.
9. What organisation do you think the poet wrote this poem for? Think carefully.

 Read the poem aloud.

1. You should notice that it changes speed. Write down why you think it does.
2. How many syllables (beats) are in the first line: 'This is the night mail crossing the border,'? Tap it out on your hand, then count the syllables on your fingers. This is the rhythm of the poem.
3. Now work out the syllables in these lines:
   (a) 'Letters for the rich, letters for the poor'
   (b) 'Dawn freshens, the climb is done.'
   (c) 'Letters of thanks, letters from banks,'
4. Put the lines in order of speed, fastest first.
5. Write down exactly why you think the poem changes speed in (a) (b) and (c) above.

 Write one of the letters mentioned in 'Night Mail'.

Look at verse III and choose which letter it will be.

D Try writing your own verse or poem which involves speed.

For example, you could be riding on your bike up and down a hill.
Experiment by tapping out a rhythm first.

The Sound of Music

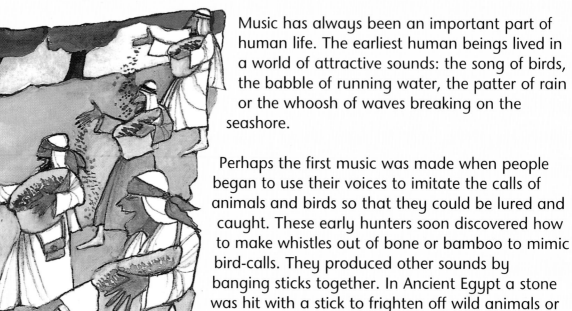

Music has always been an important part of human life. The earliest human beings lived in a world of attractive sounds: the song of birds, the babble of running water, the patter of rain or the whoosh of waves breaking on the seashore.

Perhaps the first music was made when people began to use their voices to imitate the calls of animals and birds so that they could be lured and caught. These early hunters soon discovered how to make whistles out of bone or bamboo to mimic bird-calls. They produced other sounds by banging sticks together. In Ancient Egypt a stone was hit with a stick to frighten off wild animals or to scare away birds from planted seeds.

As life became more organised, people found that music was a great help for getting through a day's work. People sang when sowing seeds, harvesting or shifting heavy loads.

For centuries, sailors sang sea-shanties on ships, while on Ancient Greek and Roman ships the slaves rowed at the oars in time to the beat of a drummer.

From earliest childhood, we hear the sounds of music all around us. Babies are sent to sleep with lullabies and small children sing their nursery rhymes to simple tunes. Throughout our modern lives music is heard on radio, cassette, compact disc and television. Films and social events such as weddings show us how music is used to affect our emotions, making us feel happy, sad, frightened or excited.

To performers and composers, music is an art. The art of music takes many forms – from the simplest tune to the biggest symphony in an orchestra, from a choir singing to the powerful beat of a rock band. Whether we prefer one kind of music to another is a matter of personal taste.

As an art, music has much in common with painting or sculpture. Like the painter or sculptor, the music composer creates a piece of work, but instead of using paint, clay or stone, he or she uses sound – The Sound of Music!

A **Answer these questions.**

1. Among what sounds did early humans live?
2. How was the first music made?
3. What materials did they use to make whistles?
4. How were animals and birds frightened away in Ancient Egypt?
5. How was sound used as life became more organised?
6. Name some emotions which music can affect?
7. How is music an 'art'?
8. How is music similar to poetry?

 B **Read paragraph six again. What kinds of musical groups are mentioned? Write them down.**

1. Choose one and think of three things you would like to know about it. For example:

   What I Would Like To Know
   A Rock Band: (a) What instruments are always in a rock band?
                 (b) _____
                 (c) _____

2. Choose another kind of musical group such as a jazz band or a steel band and write down three things you would like to know.
3. Look carefully at what you have written. Write down the best places to look for answers. (For example the library, your music teacher.)

 C **Now choose one musical group to research.**

When you have found the best places to look, make notes. If you can, present some of the information you collect as a diagram with labels, a wall chart or a writing frame.

Your writing frame could begin:
One thing I wanted to find out about _____ was _____ .
So I went to _____
The first thing I found out _____ .

The Apostrophe

- An apostrophe (') is used to show possession or ownership.

  e.g. **a.** the girl's hat   **b.** the dog's bones

- The possessing or 'owning' nouns in examples **a** and **b** are in the singular. There is one girl/one dog. The apostrophe is therefore indicated by 's. (Notice it does not matter in **a** and **b** whether the possessed or 'owned' noun, i.e. the hat, the bones, is in the singular or in the plural.)

 Rewrite the following using the apostrophe (as shown in a and b).

1. the glove of the woman
2. the photos belonging to the girl
3. the sails of the ship
4. the angry face of the bull
5. the eggs of the bird
6. the decision of the manager
7. the rocking chair belonging to Mrs Beaver
8. the pony belonging to Tess

- In the plural – as in examples **c** and **d** – the apostrophe is shown in two ways.

  c. the boys' shoes   **d.** the men's coats

1. When the plural already ends in -s, e.g. boys, ducks, we show the apostrophe as (s'), e.g. the swimmers' pool, or the girls' teachers.
2. When the plural does not end in -s, e.g. children, women etc., we show the apostrophe as ('s), e.g. the children's game, the women's marathon.

 Rewrite the following using the apostrophe (as shown in c and d).

1. the saddles of the horses
2. the eggs of the geese
3. the keys of the men
4. the air pressure of the tyres
5. the hats of the girls
6. the feathers of the swans
7. the tails of the mice
8. the prices of the books
9. the sweets of the children
10. the enemies of salmon

Overused Words – Nice/Ate

 Choose the more interesting sentence.

(a) The boys ate the nice bars of chocolate.
(b) The young boys devoured the delicious bars of creamy chocolate.

Why is the sentence you chose more interesting?

 Copy the following sentences and replace the word 'ate' with a more interesting word from the box.

gobbled	chewed	nibbled	munched	swallowed	devoured

1. The tiny mouse (*ate*) the lump of cheese.
2. Shenaz (*ate*) her apple noisily.
3. The tiger (*ate*) the meat greedily.
4. The hungry boy (*ate*) his dinner quickly.
5. The cow stared as she (*ate*) the grass.

 Insert a word from the list below in place of the word 'nice'.

wonderful	beautiful	delicious	impressive	enjoyable	interesting
pleasant	tasty	cosy	fantastic	incredible	mouth-watering	soft

1. The treacle tarts were (*nice*).
2. They live in a (*nice*) house.
3. We sat down on the (*nice*) sofa.
4. The view from the summit of the Pocano Mountains was quite (*nice*).
5. Jane has a (*nice*) display of dried flowers.
6. That night, the fireworks exploded into (*nice*) colours and (*nice*) shapes.
7. The old woman behind the counter hadn't a very (*nice*) face.

 Write down as many words as you can to describe chocolate.

sweet  sticky

59

The Sweet-shop

The sweet-shop in Llandaff in the year 1923 was the very centre of our lives. To us, it was what a bar is to a drunk, or a church to a bishop. Without it, there would have been little to live for. But it had one terrible drawback, this sweet-shop: the woman who owned it was a horror. We hated her and we had good reason for doing so.

Her name was Mrs Pratchett. She was a small skinny old hag with a moustache on her upper lip and a mouth as sour as a green gooseberry. She never smiled. She never welcomed us when we went in and the only time she spoke was when she said things like, "I'm watchin' you so keep your thievin' fingers off them chocolates!" or, "I don't want you in here just to look around! Either you forks out or you gets out!"

But by far the most loathsome thing about Mrs Pratchett was the filth that clung around her. Her apron was grey and greasy. Her blouse had bits of breakfast all over it, toast-crumbs and tea-stains and splotches of dried egg-yolk. It was her hands, however, that disturbed us most. They were disgusting. They were black with dirt and grime. They looked as though they had been putting lumps of coal on the fire all day long. And do not forget, please, that it was these very hands and fingers that she plunged into sweet-jars when we asked for a pennyworth of Treacle Toffee or Wine Gums or Nut Clusters or whatever. There were precious few health laws in those days, and nobody, least of all Mrs Pratchett, ever thought of using a little shovel for getting out the sweets as they do today. The mere sight of her grimy right hand with its black fingernails digging the Chocolate Fudge out of a jar would have caused a starving tramp to go running from the shop.

But not us. Sweets were our life-blood. We would have put up with far worse than that to get them. So we simply stood and watched in sullen silence while this disgusting old woman stirred around inside the jars with her foul fingers.

Roald Dahl

60

 A **Answer these questions.**

1. What was the very centre of the children's lives?
2. What was the drawback of the sweet-shop?
3. Why does Roald Dahl call the sweet-shop owner a 'disgusting old woman'?
4. Would you buy her sweets? Give reasons for your answer.

 B **Do you think the sweet shop was real? Decide which of these describes the account best:**

fact   fiction   fiction based on fact

Say why you have chosen your answer.

 C **Write a character sketch of Mrs Pratchett.**

Make notes first, in the same way as those on page 35.

 D **Imagine you are Mrs Pratchett.**

Write a paragraph explaining what you think of the children who come in your shop.

 E **The sweet-shop is the setting of the account. It is very important to the children: somewhere they will always remember.**

Read the account again and imagine what the sweet-shop looked like. It would be very different from the 'sour' Mrs Pratchett.

List words which could describe the sweet-shop and use them to write a description of it.

Treacle Toffee, Wine Gums, Nut Clusters, Chocolate Fudge. Think of words that rhyme with these and use them to make up names for sweets. Think of the sweets you eat and add those. Write a poem with two words to each line like this:

Treacle Toffee
Cream Coffee

_____

Give your poem an interesting title.

Christmas

 A **What do you think of when you hear the word 'Christmas'? Write down as many Christmas words as you can think of.**

B **Use these ideas to write about Christmas.**

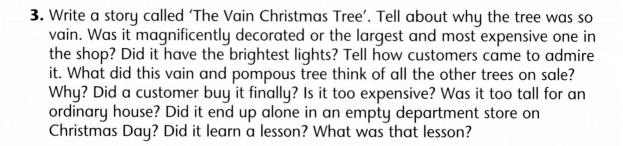

1. 'Tis the season to be jolly. However, the fairy at the top of the Christmas tree is extremely unhappy. Give reasons why you think she is feeling this way.

2. Imagine you are a Christmas cracker. Unlike your companions, who are bursting for the arrival of Christmas Day, you are dreading the whole season – particularly Christmas Day! You do not want to be pulled. Write about your thoughts and feelings and how you as a cracker will try to stop/resist the hands of people who want to break you apart!

3. Write a story called 'The Vain Christmas Tree'. Tell about why the tree was so vain. Was it magnificently decorated or the largest and most expensive one in the shop? Did it have the brightest lights? Tell how customers came to admire it. What did this vain and pompous tree think of all the other trees on sale? Why? Did a customer buy it finally? Is it too expensive? Was it too tall for an ordinary house? Did it end up alone in an empty department store on Christmas Day? Did it learn a lesson? What was that lesson?

Suffixes (4) – Changing Nouns and Verbs to Adjectives

You can add suffixes to nouns and verbs and turn them into adjectives like this:

verb   **adjective**
wash   washable

I can **wash** this jacket
This jacket is **washable**.

 A **Choose from the suffixes and turn the nouns into adjectives. Some suffixes might go with more than one word.**

ful	al	ish	able	less

season   harm   miser   comfort   fool   fever   accident   doubt   hope

How many new words did you discover?

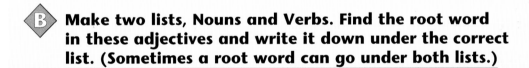 **B** **Make two lists, Nouns and Verbs. Find the root word in these adjectives and write it down under the correct list. (Sometimes a root word can go under both lists.)**

likeable   childish   crooked   suitable   heroic   shocking   talkative

 C **We can also make two words into an adjective.**

e.g. animal-loving

How many adjectives can you make with these words?
road   child   good   kind   like   hearted   worthy

D **Write a poem called 'Animal Magic'.**

Use words such as: dog-loving, cat-loving, snake-loving, animal-loving.
Think of as many animals as you can.

Making Your Writing More Interesting

Remember:

- A **full stop** ends a sentence.
- A **comma** can separate parts of a sentence.
- Words such as **and**, **but**, **because**, **with** are called **connectives**. They are used to join sentences to make one longer sentence.
  We can use these to make our writing more interesting.
- Read the following:
  I went to see the Dragon Dance yesterday. My grandmother took me. It was very exciting.
  The writing flows better if we say:
  Yesterday, my grandmother took me to see the Dragon Dance, which was very exciting.
- Now read this:
  The dragon was red and black and gold and it had huge glass eyes and they wobbled from side to side.
  It sounds better if we say:
  The dragon was red, black and gold. It had huge glass eyes, which wobbled from side to side.

 Write this title in your book: The Dragon Dance.

Copy out the two redrafted sentences above.

 Redraft these sentences using full stops, commas and connectives to make the sentences flow better then add them to the other sentences. You will make a paragraph.

Read your work through, as you go. Decide what sounds best.

1. The dragon had fire coming out of its mouth.
   The fire was made from paper streamers and feathers.
2. The fire looked as if it was dancing.
   The breeze was blowing the paper and feathers in the air.
3. I think my grandmother was frightened.
   The creature looked so fierce.

Read your finished paragraph aloud. Change it again if you need to and add more information if you want.

After We've Gone

Who will live in our house
After we've gone?
Will they have green plastic
Instead of lawn?

Who will live in our house
After the wars?
Will there be mutations
That crawl on all fours?

Will the shiny robot workers
Be dreaming strange, new dreams?
Will the pigeons, big as turkeys,
Roost on our ancient beams?

Who will use our kitchen?
What will they cook?
Who will sleep in our room?
And how will they look?

Will they feel our ghosts disturbing
Their cybernetic years
With the echoes of our laughter
And the shadows of our tears?

Will there still be lovers?
Who will sing our songs?
Who will live in our house
After we've gone?

Fran Landesman

 Answer these questions.

1. How can we tell the poet is looking into the future?
2. What does the poet see as she looks inside the house?
3. List three questions the poet asks.
4. What does the poet mean by 'After we've gone' – to another house, country? Where?
5. Do you think the poet cares about what will happen 'After we've gone'? If so, why?
6. What do you think the mood or feeling of the poet is? Does she feel happy, sad, angry, frightened? Give a reason for your answer.

 Look carefully at each verse.

1. Write down which words rhyme with each other at the end of a line, like this: Verse 1, line 2 and line 4, gone/lawn.
2. What do you notice about the rhyme in each verse? Is there a pattern? Explain.

 Look at the first verse.

How many syllables (beats) are in each line? Tap out on your hand. Then count the syllables on your fingers. Can you see any other verses which are the same?

 Write a poem, beginning each line with a question:

Who? What? Where? Why? When? How?

Paragraphs (2)

- A paragraph is a group or a collection of sentences which are gathered together to describe one main idea or one piece of action.
- Most stories will have a 'beginning', a 'middle' and an 'ending' paragraph.

 A **Choose one of these options.**

(a) You are doing some spring-cleaning/renovations/moving house ... when you discover ... in the attic/under the floorboards ...

(b) You are a collector and on examining your display ... you discover a curiosity, something rare ... You decide to get it investigated with some wonderful results ...

 B **Answer these questions. Think of some help-words for each paragraph of your story, such as those in the sacks.**

Paragraph 1
Introduce yourself.
What were you doing one day?
Where did you find your item?

Paragraph 2
Describe what you found.
How did you get more information?
How did you feel when you got it valued? (List your feelings.)

Paragraph 3
What was the value of your find?
Why was it so rare?
Who did you tell – TV, reporters, family?
What did you decide to do with your fortune?

family talk-show

millions

wonderful

enthusiast

cleaning

stamps

magnifying glass

astonished

shook off the cobwebs

Defining Words

- When we are trying to explain what a word means we often use more than one word, like this:

  A library is a place where books are kept.
- We could use fewer words and say: Where books are kept.
- At other times we could replace the word with another that has a similar meaning:

  e.g. cloudy – gloomy

 A **Use four words only to explain the meaning of these words.**

cinema	museum	calendar
search	correct	foolish

 B **Use three words only to explain the meaning of these words.**

book	bucket	narrow
bird	first	spacious

 C **Now use two words only.**

discover	accept	angry	modern
residence	annually	powerful	

 D **Replace these words with another that has a similar meaning.**

planet	clown	flower	beautiful	rascal
swing	clever	pudding	empty	rapid

 E **Decide which word fits best and write out the sentence.**

1. There was expensive old/antique furniture in the shop window.

2. The teachers had a short/brief meeting during the morning break.

3. It was a lively/bright party with lots of music and dancing.

Road Accident

1. Invent a name for the street, road or avenue.
2. Decide on a date and time of day.
3. Describe the position of the cars at the front.
4. What else can you see? What's on the road?
5. How do you think the accident happened?
6. How bad is the damage to the cars?
7. Give the police officers' names.
8. Why are they there?
9. What are they doing?
10. What equipment is being used?
11. Invent two witnesses and give them names.
12. What did they see? What did they hear – screeching of brakes? What did they do – call an ambulance, give first aid, comfort people?
13. Who were in the cars? Why did the drivers crash into each other? Were they drunk or trying to avoid an obstacle?
14. Where are the injured now? What is their condition? Who will remove the wrecked vehicles?
15. How do the witnesses feel? How do the onlookers feel?
16. Now describe the accident as if you are a witness. Listen to the witness accounts from other groups.

Options

1. Write out the details of the police officers' accident report. Use these words as headings: Incident, Vehicle description, Owner, Witnesses' statements.
2. The class must play the court where the evidence is to be heard. Elect the judge and jury. Listen to the evidence from the tapes and decide on the **facts** of the case.
3. Design a poster about 'Safety on the Roads'. What will your statement be? What message do you want to communicate to drivers, cyclists and pedestrians?

Street Musicians

10. Why did they choose to play there? Are they practising for a late performance? Are they trying to earn money ... saving for a new instrument? Are they looking for fame? Are they hoping someone important will find them? Who?

11. Look at the people in the background. Are they listening? What are they doing there?

12. Why is there some money on the bag?

13. What tells you that they are not playing for charity?

14. What are they thinking as they play?

15. Has today been a successful day?

16. What tells you that they aren't famous musicians?

17. What are their dreams for the future?

1. What are the men doing?

2. Describe their appearance.

3. Which instrument are they playing?

4. What are they sitting on?

5. What sounds can you hear?

6. What kind of music are they playing – happy, lonely, lively, classical, pop, jazz? How do you know?

7. What tells you this is not a rock band?

8. Why is it incorrect to say that they belong to an orchestra?

9. Where are they playing?

Options

1. Write a short poem entitled 'The Street Musician' or 'The Busker'.

2. Design your own advertisement for a musical concert, showing where and when it will be performed, who will play (a group or solo artist), and the cost of the ticket, of course!

3. Dramatise an encounter between one of the men in the picture and a police officer who is trying to move them on. Either prepare the dialogue or improvise.

Never-Never Land

Over the sea in the bright blue sky,
The birdies swim and the fishes fly,
The limpets dance and the lobsters sing,
And the heart is as light as a linnet's wing.

Over the sea in the bright blue sky,
The crocodiles feed on pumpkin pie,
The porpoises play with a passing moonbeam,
And the heart is as light as a summer's dream.

Over the sea in the bright blue sky,
There's never a tear, there's never a sigh,
The hours are filled with nothing wrong,
And the heart is as light as a butterfly's song.

Over the sea in the bright blue sky,
Where the birdies swim and the fishes fly,
Is the door to a land you can never unlock,
For the days are as long as a timeless clock.

Mary Green

Read through the poem on page 70 and answer these questions.

1. Why do you think the poem is called 'Never-Never Land'? Where is it?
2. In what ways are the creatures that live there different? Give three examples.
3. Why is the heart 'light'?
4. How is Never-Never Land different from the real world?
5. Why does the poem say we can never find this land?
6. Although the poem describes happiness, why is it also sad?
7. Find out the meaning of these words: limpet, linnet, pumpkin, porpoise.
8. What fairy story do you know that has a pumpkin in it?
9. Write down any words which you think describe the poem: nursery rhyme, fairy story, fantasy, nonsense poem, alphabet poem, rhyming poem. Say why.

B **Which lines rhyme at the end? Give three examples.**

Try to find a pair of words that rhyme in the middle of a line.

C **Which lines are repeated?**

D **Find four words in the first verse that begin with 's'.**

Now write down words that begin with 'l' in the first verse and 'p' in the second verse.

E **This poem has a regular beat or rhythm.**

Count the syllables in some of the lines. Try to think of a word to describe the rhythm. Make up a word if you want to.

F **Each line ends with a rhyming couplet, e.g. 'sky' and 'fly'. Make up a rhyming couplet about:**

the sea, the sky, a sunny day or one of your favourite things.
Look in the poem for ideas.

G **Write your own poem about an imaginary land.**

You can write a poem with a regular beat or rhythm like this one if you like – it's up to you! Write down all your ideas before you start.

Island Expedition

1. Make up a name for the place in the picture.

2. What time of day is it?

3. What are the people on the boat there for? Are they working? Are they sight-seeing? Are they travelling?

4. What is the weather like? How does the sea look?

5. What is the man who is standing on the front of the boat doing? Is he a tourist?

6. Look at the boat in the background. Is it the same as the other boat? Describe the differences.

7. Would you like to swim in the water? Why?

Options

1. Imagine you are a reporter for a travel programme. You have travelled to this place and spent a few days there. Give your report to the TV camera. Is it good or bad?

2. You are exploring the island with a friend and find a secret beach. What do you find there? Maybe it's a band of criminals or buried treasure.

3. Design a poster advertising the island. What words could you use to describe it – sunny, quiet, lively, clear sea, clean beaches?

Fox Hunting

Justin has written this letter to his friend Simon.

> 4 Market Street
> Mayling
> Malthamshire
> 8 July 1998
>
> Dear Simon
>
> I have something surprising – and upsetting – to tell you. It happened a few days ago.
>
> Last Saturday Dean, my brother, and I were playing on the swing in our local woods. When my turn came, I tried to swing as high as I could. No, I didn't fall off, but I did catch sight of an animal lying on the ground some distance away. I could only just see it, so we decided to go and investigate. It was a fox which had been torn to shreds by hounds. My brother said he could tell how it had died. It's tail was long and bushy and a beautiful colour, but the rest of it was a terrible sight! My brother says that fox are vermin and the hunt destroys them, but I don't think it can be right to kill an animal in this way. He says they sometimes remove the animal once the hounds have finished with it, but I'm glad I've seen this. It's made me think about fox hunting and what a painful death the fox must have had.
>
> What do you think about fox hunting? Does it make you feel angry or do you agree with my brother? Please write soon and let me know.
>
> Your good friend
>
> Justin

 Answer these questions.

1. How do you know Justin lives in the country?
2. When did Justin go to the woods?
3. What did Justin see?
4. Why was it a terrible sight?
5. What did Justin's brother say?
6. Why has Justin written to his friend Simon?

 Find out more about fox hunting.

Then pretend you are Simon and write a reply to Justin, explaining your views about fox hunting. Set your letter out properly.

Confusing Words (3)

A Read the examples, then copy these sentences inserting **were** or **where**.

● **where/were**

'Where' means 'what place'.

e.g. Where is the best place to see dinosaur bones?

'Were' is from the verb 'to be'. It is the plural of 'was'.

e.g. Dinosaurs were huge monsters.

1. _____ did you go last night?
2. _____ there many elephants in the jungle?
3. They _____ at a football match two days ago.
4. We didn't know _____ the teachers _____ .
5. We _____ standing _____ the river was flowing and skimming pebbles along the water's surface.

B Read the examples, then copy these sentences inserting **our** or **are**.

● **are/our**

'Are' is from the verb 'to be'. It is the plural of 'is'; e.g. They are enjoying the party.

'Our' means 'belonging to us'; e.g. They thought our party was best.

1. May we introduce you to _____ parents, Steve and Mary.
2. Where are _____ bags?
3. They _____ coming over to _____ house later this evening.
4. _____ American relatives _____ planning to visit _____ country soon.

C Read the examples, then copy these sentences inserting **it's** or **its**.

● **it's/its**

'it's' means it is. e.g. It's a lovely day.

'its' (without the ') means 'belonging to'. e.g. The doll is wearing its hat.

1. The canary is singing in _____ cage.
2. The windows are open because _____ a hot day.
3. ' _____ not fair,' moaned Paul.
4. The dog is burying _____ bone.
5. _____ dangerous to cross the road when _____ busy.

Question Marks

● Always begin a question with a capital letter and end it with a question mark (?).
e.g. What did you do? Where did you go? Why weren't you back an hour ago?

 Insert the missing capital letters and question marks in these questions.

1. __hat is a computer
2. __hen was the computer a monster of a machine
3. __hy has the computer shrunk in size
4. __s the computer a thinking machine
5. __here are they widely used
6. __hich kind of computer do you use
7. __ow does it work
8. __hat controls the robots
9. __hen will we have computerised alarm-clocks

 Write down questions for these answers.

1. He lived with his mother and father.
2. In a beautiful house beside the sea.
3. There was the sandy beach to run on and the ocean to paddle in.
4. James' mother and father went to London.
5. They went to do some shopping.
6. They were eaten up by an enormous angry rhinoceros.
7. James found himself alone and frightened.
8. Aunt Sponge and Aunt Spiker were his two horrible aunts.
9. He cried because he was overwhelmed by his own unhappiness.
10. The skin of the peach was very beautiful – a rich buttery yellow with patches of brilliant pink and red.

Can you think of which story these answers were taken from and who the author of that book is?

C **Write two questions that each of these people might ask.**

1. A doctor	4. A customer	7. A parent to a child
2. A tourist	5. A teacher	8. A child to a parent
3. A motorist	6. A police officer	9. A school inspector

Letter Strings

You can remember spellings by grouping words of the same letter string together. This is very useful for words which look similar but do not sound the same.

A **Write two headings in your book: oul and ou.**

Put these words under the correct heading.

should   country   could   trouble

couple   cousin   would

shoulder   young   double

B **Work with a partner. Write sentences for words your partner is not sure of. (Choose no more than three.)**

Your sentences should show the meaning of the words.
Dictate them to your partner.
Now swap over.

Mark each other's work to see if the words are spelled correctly.
Record the words you forget easily with a word of the same letter pattern that you know well.

C **Now do the same with these letter patterns: ough and our.**

rough   through   hour

course   pour   journey   four

ought   bought   dough

your   tourist

flour   nourish   flourish   our

plough   borough   though   cough

D **Can you find any words which rhyme?**

Market Stalls

1. What is the name of the street? (Invent one.)

2. What kind of a street is it?

3. Describe what is on sale.

4. What day is it? What time is it?

5. Describe the scene. What sounds do you hear? What do you smell? What are people doing? Describe the hustle and bustle.

6. Describe the man looking at the camera. Who is he? What is he selling today? What is he doing right now?

7. Describe the woman on the left of the picture. How does she look – happy, sad, thoughtful, angry, busy? Where do you think she is going?

8. Look again at the man on the card stall. What is he thinking?

9. The man must sell all he can today. What does he say to the shoppers? How does he say it?

10. What would he say to: a cranky customer, a haughty shopper, a fuss-pot, a bold child, a cheeky teenager?

11. What are the shoppers' comments or remarks to each other as they pass?

12. What other stalls are out of view but on the same street today?

13. When will they shut down/close?

Options

1. Select a stall for each member of the group. Invent a chant or patter to encourage people to buy things from each stall. If there is time, record each one on to tape to play to the class. Alternatively, learn your patter by heart to share with them at the end of the session.

2. Set up a dialogue between a stallholder and a customer. Rehearse it and tape-record the results to share with the class.

Words with Common Roots

- A root word is a simple word or unit. Prefixes and suffixes are added to roots to make new words. Sometimes we can see the whole root word, at other times only part of it.
- Root words, prefixes and suffixes are usually part of older languages such as Latin (L) and Greek (G).

A <u>**Group all the words with the same roots together and write them down.**</u>

advent	press-up	answerphone	pressure
prevent	depress	telephone	press	microphone

Underline the root word.

B <u>**Work out the meaning of the words in A and where they come from, using the following information:**</u>

(L) venio = I come   (L) pressus = pressed   (G) phone = sound

C <u>**Now do the same with the following:**</u>

aquarium	rotate	navy	rotund
rotation	aqueduct	octagon	octahedron	navigate

(G) okto = (L) octo = eight   (L) aqua = water
(L) navis = a ship   (L) rota = a wheel

D <u>**Find words in your dictionary which have the same root word as these:**</u>

revolve   describe   manual   dinosaur

E <u>**Some words can be made up of a prefix and a suffix.**</u>
<u>**Find the origin of these words in a dictionary:**</u>

hemisphere   subway   kilogram

Out of Tune

 A **Write down as many sounds as you can think of when you look at the picture.**

Bleat Thump Howl Rumble Thud

 B **Read the following passage.**

The most important and biggest concert of the year was only three days away. For hours the musicians practised their pieces and were happy and confident that all would go perfectly well on the 'big night'. Their musical instruments, however, were far from happy and between practice sessions they began to complain and grumble about their tough life and how they felt overplayed, tired and worn out. Together as an orchestra they decided on a plan to show just how dissatisfied they were. When? On the night of the 'Big Concert' of course! How? By sounding slightly 'out of tune'!

 C **Use the questions below to help you organise the paragraphs of this story.**

- **Paragraph 1.** Where was the concert to be held? When? Why was it going to be the most important/biggest concert ... ? Who would be there – royalty, the President, film stars? (Use names.)
- **Paragraph 2.** For how long did the musicians practise? Can you name some of their musical pieces and the composers? How did the musicians feel? What instruments did they play? List them. How did their instruments feel? When did they begin to complain? Why? What was their problem?
- **Paragraph 3.** What did they plan to do? How would they sound 'out of tune'? What sounds did they play on the night of the concert? What did each instrument do – bark, grunt, howl, screech? Did the musicians or the audience expect this?
- **Paragraph 4.** How did all the people react? What did they hear? How did they feel? What did they say? Did they laugh, scream, faint, run, hide ... ? How did the instruments feel? Were they triumphant?

 D **Can you think of another title for the story?**

The Complaining Instruments ...

Escape at Bedtime

The lights from the parlour and the kitchen shone out
Through the blinds and the windows and bars;
And high overhead and all moving about,
There were thousands and thousands of stars,
There ne'er were such thousands of leaves on a tree,
Nor of people in church or the park,
As the crowds of the stars that looked down upon me
And that glittered and winked in the dark.

The Dog and The Plough and The Hunter and all,
And the star of the sailor and Mars,
These shone in the sky, and the pail by the wall
Would be half full of water and stars.
They saw me at last and they chased me with cries,
And they soon had me perched into bed.
But the glory kept shining and bright in my eyes
And the stars going round in my head.

Robert Louis Stevenson

 A **Answer these questions.**

1. What lines tell us that it is night-time?
2. What did the poet see in the sky?
3. Describe the stars as the poet saw them.
4. What words or phrases tell us that the stars were in large numbers?
5. Give the names of the constellations that the poet recognised.
6. How could 'the pail by the wall' be 'half full of water and stars'?
7. Where do you think the poet should have been instead of going out to look at the stars?
8. What do you think he thought of the stars? Use a word or a phrase from the poem in your answer.
9. What do you think he dreamed about that night?
10. Write a short poem or story called 'I Followed a Star'.

    Mention when this happened, where you went and what happened. Did you settle on another planet? Did you meet a 'Starship Enterprise'? Did you meet aliens? What happened on your return to Earth?

Making a Call

1. What does the verb 'to communicate' mean?

2. Mention ways in which people are able to communicate with each other nowadays.

3. Where are the people in the photo?

4. What are they doing?

5. Describe the woman in the nearest telephone box? What is: her name, her age, her appearance? What is she – a student, tourist, doctor?

6. Who is she talking to – her mother, her friend, her boyfriend ... ?

7. Why is she having a conversation with that person?

8. Describe the man in the next telephone box. Who is he? What is his age, his appearance? What is his career – nurse, salesman, criminal, detective, scientist ... ?

9. Who is he going to communicate with? Why?

10. Describe the older man in the background. Who is he? What is his appearance? Is he a judge, a librarian, a cleaner? Perhaps he has a day off today?

11. He is deep in conversation with someone. Who is it – a daughter, a friend?

12. Why did he call that person?

13. How does each of these people feel? Are they having pleasant conversations? Could they be quarrelling? How do you know? Look at their faces.

Options

Here are three occasions when a telephone might be important. Select one option and choose someone to play the caller and another to receive the call.

1. You see a fire in a house across the road.

2. You find your grandma collapsed at the foot of the stairs in her house.

3. You have gone on a school camping holiday and must let your parents know how it is going.

A Strange Customer

The red-faced smith was like a friendly giant. He was the biggest and strongest man in the village and was always cheerful. When he laughed, his eyes danced in the firelight. He seemed to fear nothing.

All the villagers liked him. Often the ringing of his hammer woke them in the morning. But there was something strange about him too. People said he had a magic hammer, which could make iron sing. His forge was a secret sanctuary where, with the help of the fire, he made the hard metal obey his will. With his hammer, he made swords for the warriors, axes for the woodsmen and ploughs for the farmers. The craft had been passed down in the family over many years. He believed that the gods had taught his ancestors to shape red-hot iron on an anvil to make weapons from it, weapons which had helped the Celts in battles against other peoples whose weapons were of softer metal. The forge was always hot and he often worked until evening if he was busy.

Once when clearing up after a long day, a tall, strong-looking man carrying a large axe came to his door. The smith noticed that the edge of the axe was damaged. The man held it out and asked the smith to mend it. Although it was late he felt, somehow, that he should not keep this stranger waiting. He placed the axe-head into the hottest part of the fire and when it was ready to work, he carried it over to the anvil with tongs. Under the force of his hammer, the metal bonded back together.

Dawn was breaking as the stranger took his axe away. Why had the smith worked all night to mend the axe? Perhaps he thought it was better to be safe than sorry. He knew that a cruel god called Esus lived in the forest. Men were sacrificed to him and he would cut the trees down with his terrible axe.

When people asked why he had been working all night, he simply said that he had been doing a job for a special customer.

Answer these questions.

1. Describe the smith.
2. What would wake the villagers in the morning?
3. What did they think was strange about the smith?
4. What kinds of jobs did he do with his hammer?
5. What metal did he work with?
6. What task did he have to do unexpectedly one evening?
7. Why do you think the smith worked all night to mend the axe?
8. Who do you think was the 'special' customer? Why?
9. Do you really believe that the smith's hammer was a 'magic' one? Give a reason for your answer.

 In the story 'A Strange Customer' the smith worked with iron. What is the name given to this kind of smith?

 Can you work out what these smiths do?

Goldsmith   Silversmith   Locksmith   Tinsmith

 Use your dictionary to help you find the meanings of these words.

ancestors   sanctuary   forge   sacrificed   warrior   craft

Put four of the above words into sentences of your own.

 Wordfinder.

List words under each heading below. Use the story to help you.

People	Adjectives	Verbs
customer	special	sacrificed

 What happened next?

Write a few paragraphs about what might have happened to the stranger. Did he fight the cruel god? Was his axe magical? Maybe he is cruel himself or a hero? You decide.

The Table Quiz

- You are the best 'human thinking-machine' among your classmates. One day you propose the idea of having a 'Table Quiz' against another class in the school.
- The proceeds of the quiz will be used to buy a state-of-the-art computer for your school.

  Put on your thinking cap and use the questions and hints below to help you organise the paragraphs of your story.

Paragraph 1

Your introduction. Who were you with? Where were you – in the library, yard, or eating lunch? What were you discussing? What did you see as the main problem? What was your idea? What were your friends' reactions to your proposal – horror, amazement, laughter, enthusiasm, excitement?

Paragraph 2

What preparations had to be made? You and your friends now had a challenge and a purpose. Explain what they were. From whom did you have to ask permission – teachers, head teacher, parents? How did the adults feel about it? What help did you need? How many teams were involved? How many on each team? Did you have raffle tickets or spot prizes ... Who prepared the questions? How many were there? Give some sample questions. Refer to history, geography, a few mathematics definitions, general knowledge ... ? Remember that those who composed the questions were not on any team.

Paragraph 3

Where was the quiz held – in the hall, a large classroom? When was it held? Who kept the scores? How long did it last? Talk about how friends, cheered or booed. Talk about the atmosphere: noise, excitement, anticipation, anxiety ... . How much money was raised? Tell about your new school computer, how you and your friends felt. Tell about what use you made of the new computer, e.g. educational games. What might your next big idea be? Who knows? You're still 'thinking' about it!

Oriental Extravaganza

1. Where is the scene taking place?
2. What event is taking place – a drama, opera, magic show, wizardry... ?
3. What can you see in the background?
4. Describe the person in the foreground. Is it easy to tell what he really looks like? Why not? What is hiding his 'real-life' features? Why is he hiding them?
5. What words would you use to describe their clothes?

   Why are they dressed like this – to frighten, for colour, to be seen ... ?
6. What is he – a conjuror or magician, a witch doctor, a clown, an actor?
7. What is he saying? How is he saying it?
8. His arms are outstretched. Who is he talking to?
9. Why are the other two people there? Could they be his assistants?
10. What do you think he will do next –

a trick, faint, magic, disappear, trip, a cartwheel or somersault, a spell?

11. How will the audience react? What will they see? What will they do? What will they say? How will they feel?

Options

1. You have a magic coat or a costume. Say what magic things happen every time you wear it.
2. You are an assistant on stage. There is also another assistant. You are both sawn in half but unfortunately your body-halves get swapped around. What happens? How do you control your movements? Can you be re-arranged again?

Using Punctuation

- A **dash** is like a comma, but is a sharper pause. We use it when we want to stress a point.

  E.g. Your tea will be ready – in two seconds.
- A **colon** is often used before you list information. It is a clear stop.

  E.g. Lay out the equipment: bowl, spoon, knife and chopping board.

  Did you notice how the comma has been used to separate the items in the list?
- A **semicolon** can be used to separate two pieces of information that are next to each other. The second part usually adds information to the first part.

  E.g. He wore a silk shirt; it was made of deep green silk.
- A **hyphen** is a short line which turns two words to make one.

  E.g. link-up

 Read the work below and decide on the correct punctuation. Check you understand by referring to the explanations above.

Write out these sentences putting in the missing dash or dashes.

   1. Goodbye remember to give my love to Dad.

   2. Send her the card the one with the jokes on it.

Pair the following words to make single words. Use the hyphen.

looking   long   liked   home   haired   grown   good   well

 Write lists about two of the following. Use colons and commas.

Packing a suitcase for a holiday.

Buying a list of groceries.

Listing the contents of your school bag.

Putting away your games and toys.

 Write out these sentences putting in the semicolon.

   1. My brother plays football he usually scores a goal.

   2. The bike was well looked after the car was in need of repair.

   3. It was an exciting match it was a match I won't forget easily.

Singular and Plural (2)

 A **Change these words into plurals.**

monastery	piano	city	Celt
loaf	knife	mouse	penny
tomato	monkey	echo	woman
hero	goose	valley	chief
gas	brother	shelf	tombstone
toothache	prince	foot	tooth

 B **Give the plural of these words.**

mouse-trap	by-law	cupful	bridegroom
onlooker	spoonful	fireman	hanger-on
mouthful	postbox	son-in-law	in-law
postman	passer-by	byway	

 C **Use your dictionary to find the plural of these words.**

syllabus	apex	gymnasium
axis	fungus	index
curriculum	cactus	appendix

 D **These words are usually used in the plural. Unscramble their letters to find out what they are. The first letter is underlined.**

sicosrss	swollag	sierlp	sarehs
wollebs	gonts	stanp	dillabrsi
belsamhs	skathn	lescepstac	resourts
lesames	zeewrest	duss	

Confusing Words (4)

 Look at the example, then write the following sentences, insert *to*, *two* or *too*.

- **To/Two/Too.**
  - e.g. **(a)** Hilda will learn how *to* play the guitar.
  - **(b)** She already owns *two* tin-whistles.
  - **(c)** She does not find her music exercises *too* difficult.

1. At first, Jane blew _____ hard when learning _____ play the recorder.
2. Billy complains that he always has _____ much homework _____ do.
3. Wilma is able _____ play a tune or _____ on her keyboard now.
4. _____ heads are better than one.
5. The piano was far _____ expensive _____ buy.

 Look at the following examples, then write out the following sentences correctly.

- **Did/Done.**
(a) 'Done' must always be used with words such as: 'has', 'have', 'was', 'is', 'are', 'were', e.g. **1.** His homework is done.   **2.** He has done his homework.
(b) 'Did' can stand alone, e.g. He did his homework.

1. Where (*did/done*) you leave your money?
2. She (*did/done*) not know if he had (*did/done*) his music homework.
3. Dad (*did/done*) the cooking while Mum (*did/done*) her painting.
4. What have you (*did/done*) with my pencil?
5. I've (*did/done*) all I'm going to do.

 Has/Have.

Write the sentences correctly using 'has' or 'have'.
1. As an art, music (*has/have*) much in common with painting.
2. The world (*has/have*) many attractive sounds.
3. We (*has/have*) to meet the composer and she (*has/have*) to meet the performer.
4. A minim (*has/have*) two beats and crochets (*has/have*) only one.
5. The opera singer must (*has/have*) years of training.
6. Orchestras (*has/have*) many musicians who (*has/have*) to play their instruments to critical audiences.

School Outing

1. What are these children doing? What is the weather like? What tells you this?

2. Where are these children going do you think – to the zoo, a farm, a fun park, a beach? Describe the place where they might be going.

3. Do they look excited, happy or bored? Why are they feeling this way?

4. What day is it – a holiday, a Saturday or a school day? What time is it?

5. What are the children thinking? E.g. 'I hope we leave soon ...', 'I hope we go to ... '.

6. What are the adults saying to the children?

7. What are the children saying to each other?

8. Have you ever been on a school trip? Where did you go? What did you see? How did you feel before and after you went? What was the weather like?

Options

1. Write a short poem entitled 'The Farm Trip'.

2. Write a story about a school trip that goes wrong. It could be due to the weather, someone going missing, everyone getting lost.

3. Write a conversation between a teacher and a boy who has forgotten to take his lunch on a trip.

Rainforest

Mary Green

Forms of Poetry

Here lieth William Wyeth
Who liveth and dieth.

A bag of bones,
Is Mr Jones,
Under these stones.

Here lies the Dodo
For whom there was no go.

Epitaph on a Bath
Here lies Duds,
Who drowned in suds,
Glug, glug.

It's not the cough that carries you off,
It's the coffin they carry you off in.

Anon

Raindrop

This
trick
le
of
rain
slips
slides
slith
ers
and
stops.
Slips
again
and
s
l
o
w
l
y
d
r
o
p
s
s
o
s
l
o
w
l
y
d
r
o
p
s
d
o
w
n
d
o
w
n
d
o
w
n
my
win
dow
pane.

Mary Green

Suppertime
Grey teeth and green gums,
A bell echoing toothache,
A coffin swallowed.

Andy Brown

There was a fine family of fleas
Who lived in the wild Pyrenees,
"How they squeeze and they tease,"
Said the trees to the breeze,
"Please, blow them away with a sneeze."

91

● Look at the poems on pages 90–91.

A **Read the definitions below and work out what each poem is. A poem could be more than one kind.**

Shape poem – A poem where the layout of the word reflects the subject.
Haiku – A poem with 3 lines and 17 syllables in total in the pattern 5, 7, 5.
Epitaph – The words put on someone's gravestone.
Rhyming couplet – Two lines, one after the other, that rhyme.
Limerick – A poem with five lines: two long ones that rhyme, then two short ones that rhyme, then a long one that rhymes with the first two.

B **Look at the shape poems carefully.**

1. How many birds are mentioned? Are there any other creatures? Write down some words that make up the trees.
2. Why is the poem 'Raindrop' shaped the way it is?
3. Now try writing your own shape poem on any theme you like.

C **Look at the haiku.**

1. How many syllables does it have? How many in each line?
2. Try to write your own. Remember to count the syllables.

D **Look at the limerick about fleas.**

1. How many lines does it have? Find another limerick in your classroom. How is it the same as this one? Check how many lines it has and where it rhymes.
2. Write your own limerick.

E **Look at the epitaphs.**

Why do they often begin 'Here lies ... '?

F **Some of the poems use words which have double meanings (a word which has two meanings). Find an example.**

Suffixes (5)

If you need to, look back at pages 32–33 to remind yourself what suffixes are.
Here are some more suffixes.

Suffix	Example
-able, -ible	changeable, edible
-ive	aggressive
-wards	upwards
-ly	politely
-tion, -sion	creation, supervision

 Choose the correct suffix: tion or sion.

1. Steve was sure they were going in the wrong *(direcsion, direction)*.
2. Imran's *(invention, invension)* was a very life-like robot.
3. Leicester railway *(station, stasion)* is really busy.
4. Mrs Coleman could not leave her class without *(supervision, supervition)*.
5. Tanya's *(predicsion, prediction)* proved to be true.

 Form new words by adding -able or -ible to the following words. You may need to change the spelling of some of them.

accept   person
exhaust   suit
sense   digest
forgive   conceive
eat

 Choose the correct suffix each time, so that the sentence makes sense.

1. The clown certainly wasn't very *(sensible, senseless)*.
2. The change in the weather is very *(noticely, noticeable)*.
3. The rocket zoomed *(uppity, upwards)* into the sky.
4. The thief *(secretly, secretive)* stole the diamonds.
5. The shuttle is very *(expensible, expensive)* to produce.

Extending Sentences

- Short simple sentences can be made more interesting by adding suitable words and phrases.
- One of the best ways of doing this is by answering one of these questions. When? Where? How? Why? Which? What kinds? e.g.

1. We went to a show. Which one?
2. We went to a magic show. When?
3. We went to a magic show when we had played enough party games.
4. The magician had some scarves. What kinds?
5. The magician had some starred and satin scarves. Where?
6. The magician had some starred and satin scarves in silver pots.
7. He performed many tricks. How?
8. He performed many tricks skillfully.
9. We applauded. Why?
10. We applauded because the magic show was over.

 Extend the following sentences by answering the questions.

1. They played games. Who?
2. They played games. Where?
3. They played games. When?
4. They played games. What kinds?
5. The magician amused the children. How?
6. They ate sausage rolls, sandwiches and other treats. When?
7. They ate sausage rolls, sandwiches and other treats. Where?
8. There was a party and a magic show. Why?
9. They left when the tricks were over. How?

- We often use 'and' or 'but' to join two sentences, e.g.
1. She came into the room (and) she waved her magic wand.
2. The door was shut tightly (but) somehow he managed to open it.

 Join the sentences together by using 'and' or 'but'.

1. I remember meeting him. I cannot remember his name.
2. We had some treats. We played games later.
3. Most cats have a tail. The Manx cat has none.
4. Witches scare me. Wizards don't.

94

Advertising

 A **Read the following advertisements and answer the questions underneath.**

Remember Gettaglow!
Forget bad-hair days!

Are you ready for
your Chokalot Chocs?

Buy
three,
get one
free!

You'll carry more
with Carymore's
carrier bags ...

Strong.
Durable.
Light.

  1. What are they advertising?

  2. List the different ways in which they advertise their goods. (For example:
     pictures, rhymes.)

  3. What do you think advertising is for? Choose from the points below and write
     them down.

     (a) to encourage people to share their belongings; (b) to sell goods

     (c) to show you how to make things; (d) for giving away goods

Check your answer is correct. Add a sentence about what else you think
advertising is for.

 B **Advertisers think about who will buy the goods they are advertising and
keep in mind certain groups of people. These are called target groups.**

  1. Who are the target groups in the adverts above – men, women ... who?

  2. Look up the word persuade in a dictionary. Why is this word used to describe
     adverts?

 C **Watch adverts on television.**

  1. Note who is doing what. For example, how are children presented?

  2. What kinds of things are women usually doing? What kinds of things are men
     usually doing? Do they do the same things or are they different?

  3. Are there any adverts which show people doing things they wouldn't usually do?

 D **Make up an advert, as a poster, in which the person in
it is doing something we wouldn't usually link them with.**

(For example: a woman flying a plane, rather than washing the dishes.)

At the Airport

1. Where are the people? (Invent a name for the airport.)
2. Where in the airport do you think these people are?
3. What details tell you that this is so? Look closely.
4. What do we call 'people' at an airport?
5. Why are some people looking at the screens?
6. What are the other people doing?
7. What sounds can be heard in the building – flight announcements ... ?
8. What kinds of conversations are people having?
9. How do they feel – tired, excited, bored, happy ... ? Why are they feeling this way?
10. Where are they going to be soon? Where have they come from? Name countries ...) (Give the passengers' names ...)
11. Why are they here? For a holiday or on business?
12. How long will they stay? Who will they see or meet?
13. What have they brought with them – luggage, duty free, gifts ... ?
14. Where will they stay – hotel, with cousins, aunt, apartment with pool?
15. What will they do – relax, swim, sunbathe, travel, sightsee, work ... ?

Options

1. Imagine you and your family have just won a 'dream-holiday' on a beautiful sun-drenched island. Write about all the things you saw, people you met. Were there any disasters or adventures?
2. Your aunt, whom you haven't seen for a long time, is coming home to stay for the summer holidays. Write about 'The Homecoming'. Was she as you expected her to be – or was she very different?